SELF-SEEKING AND THE PURSUIT OF JUSTICE

Self-Seeking and the Pursuit of Justice

DAVID P. LEVINE
Graduate School of International Studies
University of Denver

Routledge
Taylor & Francis Group
LONDON AND NEW YORK

First published 1997 by Ashgate Publishing

Reissued 2018 by Routledge
2 Park Square, Milton Park, Abingdon, Oxon, OX14 4RN
52 Vanderbilt Avenue, New York, NY 10017

Routledge is an imprint of the Taylor & Francis Group, an informa business

A Library of Congress record exists under LC control number: 97073205

ISBN 13: 978-1-138-34280-4 (hbk)
ISBN 13: 978-0-429-43956-8 (ebk)

Contents

Acknowledgements

I would like to thank Nawfal Umari, Richard Winfield, and Ross Zucker for comments on an earlier draft of this essay. I would also like to thank Chris Thurner for his assistance in the preparation of the section on economic democracy.

Preface

We most often call upon the language of justice when, as individuals or in groups, we feel deprived of something assumed to be rightfully ours. Use of this language interprets our situation as one involving the experience of loss, while attributing loss to the action of others, who become responsible for it. Those who experience loss demand justice, which is to say, they insist either on replacing what has been lost, or imposing a comparable loss on those held responsible.

Deprivation is sometimes thought to be instantiated in institutions, which are seen as mechanisms by which a loss is imposed on some for the benefit of others. Then, justice and injustice are no longer simply about interpersonal interaction, but about the design of institutions, and of the forces that shape those institutions. Just institutions are those that do not allow interactions by which some benefit from the deprivation of others. Unjust institutions make such outcomes inevitable. The justness of economic institutions is sometimes interpreted this way, particularly by those who favor a notion of exploitation. Exploitation, as Marx uses the term, is not a matter of individual willing, but of institutions that shape and determine action that results in the product becoming the property of someone other than the worker who produced it. Though Marx does not do so, it would be possible to use the notion of exploitation to distinguish just from unjust institutions.

Two problems arise in this use of language. The first is the necessity that our loss be treated as deprivation. Clearly some losses do result from deprivation; but, many do not, or only appear to in light of a specific interpretation. Thus, deprivation becomes a matter of interpretation. The second problem is the impetus in the language of justice to think that replacing our loss is possible, and that blaming others, and shifting the loss onto them, is one of the appropriate means. This way of thinking and talking about justice leads to interpretations based on notions of deprivation and rectification, rather than on a positive idea of how human interaction can foster self-determination, and that many sided development of the individual once alluded to by Marx.

Are just institutions those that shift the burden of loss from one individual or group to another, for example through punishment or through redistribution; or are just institutions those that secure self-determination, so far as that is possible? The two meanings interconnect around the issue of deprivation, since both understand that justice concerns itself with deprivation. One focuses on the negative side: how to rectify past deprivation. The other focuses on the positive side: how to secure the individual from the experience of deprivation. Of the two, rectification carries the greater salience; it is the one that provokes the strongest feelings, and that makes the term justice bear the heaviest burden. Sensitivity to deprivation has reached remarkable heights, as individuals and groups make demands for rectification, and, more and more frequently, seek to place responsibility for their losses (real and imagined) on others. At the center of this proliferation of blame lies the idea that losses can be put right. Thus, the proliferation of blame goes hand in hand with a proliferation of claims about rights, so that we experience ever expanding demands for new rights.

The pursuit of justice as rectification for past deprivation does not, however, so much resolve the problem of deprivation as keep it alive by passing it along from individual to individual, group to group. This is because deprivation that matters is rarely, if ever, put right. What can be done, and affords a more realistic and promising opportunity for justice, is the prevention of future deprivation, and thus of the need for rectification. This involves focusing our attention on the design of social institutions that minimize deprivation.

To know what institutions instantiate justice, we must be able to answer the question: What is the deprivation against which justice seeks to make the individual secure? In the following, I take the answer to this question to center around the idea of the self. What we are deprived of, and what justice seeks to prevent our deprivation of, is a specific self-feeling and self-experience. This is the self-feeling and experience necessary to autonomy. In part, we gain this feeling from being afforded the opportunity to be ourselves, to express who we are in the world, and to pursue our self-interest. Just institutions assure, so far as possible, that we can define and pursue our self-interest in a world of others.

Here, I consider only one aspect of the problem of the justness of social institutions, the aspect bearing on economic institutions. Economic institutions have to do with the production and use of wealth: with how much wealth is and can be produced, and how, by whom, and for what, it gets used. This, then, is an essay on wealth and justice, and how wealth can best be put in the service of justice. My concern is less, however, with specific recommendations than with the underlying normative considerations that would make specific policies lead in the direction of justice. In this sense, the essay is preliminary in nature, though I make some more practical suggestions along the way.

1 Justice and interests

Justice

We can speak of justice in different ways that connect it to different defining terms: justice as equality, justice as dueness, justice as fairness, justice as impartiality, and justice as respect for rights.[1] Each association tells us something about justice, though the different terms carry somewhat different connotations and, perhaps, express the different ethos particular authors seek to evoke.

Of course it may matter whether we are most concerned with economic justice, or with justice's other aspects. Traditionally, economic justice has been about distribution, so concepts such as fairness, dueness, and equality seem to apply more directly than impartiality: fairness in the allocation of amounts among persons, or more generally in the way those amounts are determined, dueness in that the amount is fair because it was in some sense earned, or equality of distribution because we think this is fair or ultimately what we are due. Distributive justice is, indeed, of special importance in judging economic organization.[2] Yet, restricting the concern of economic justice in this way leaves many fundamental issues untouched. Those issues have to do not only with who gets how much, but with the kind of relationships through which each acquires the means for satisfying wants, with the kinds of wants that get satisfied (especially the relation of want to individuation), and with the limits of private want and its satisfaction. A just economy is not simply one where each gains what is in some sense the appropriate amount of income and wealth, although presumably a just economy accomplishes this end. To be just, the economy must also sustain a special form of interaction, one that secures the appropriate regard for personhood we associate with impartiality and respect for rights. In a broader consideration of justice and the economy, none of the aspects of justice suggested by the defining terms -- equality, dueness, fairness, impartiality, and right -- can be ignored.

Speaking of justice surely invokes the idea of equality; but the kind of equality implied in justice is less clear. And, indeed, the notion of equality is notoriously elusive (see Williams 1962). In economic affairs, equality of outcome conflicts with equality of opportunity, at least in the context of market economy. Greater equality along one dimension may mean less along another; so we cannot really say whether equality as such is served.

The notion of dueness takes us a step forward by allowing for the income differences that cause trouble in arguments resting on equality. That each gets what is due him (or her) implies a kind of equality, but not the equality of income sometimes implied in the demand for more justice.[3] Getting your due is consistent with significant inequalities of income and wealth. Then, to get something other than what is your due would be unjust even if it is more equal.

Fairness, at least in John Rawls's sense, need not imply equality or dueness, or even impartiality, though it retains elements of those ideas. To favor the worst off might or might not lead to greater equality of income across persons. Arguments in economics since Adam Smith suggest otherwise. These arguments support the claim that inequality benefits the worst off by acting as an incentive system for investment, innovation, and the growth of social wealth. At the same time, fairness that means favoring the worst off is not impartial in any simple sense. Nor is there any obvious link between fairness defined this way and dueness, especially if dueness is in some way linked to contribution.[4]

Defining (economic) justice as limiting inequalities of income and wealth to those that benefit the worst off seeks justice under conditions where wealth is in some sense scarce. Justice as fairness, in this meaning of the term, has to do with the justness of arrangements that, because of this condition, cannot be fair in any stronger sense. Thus, for example, were justice to require the satisfaction of wants, as I will suggest further on, we could not find justice in a world where scarcity prevails, since scarcity means that some wants will not be satisfied.

Whether this means we should change our definition of justice remains to be determined. Justice as fairness seeks to find justice in a world of scarcity, though it does not first establish that the condition of scarcity is consistent with the pursuit of justice. This, then, applies the concept of justice to situations where justice is limited by externally given conditions.

Justice defines an ideal arrangement. Achieving justice means organizing institutions to achieve a normative end. The ideal of justice is part of our effort to remake our world rather than take it as we find it. This project is the more compelling because the world as we find it falls short of our ideal. Those conditions that assure the world falls short of the ideal are external in that their origin must be sought elsewhere than in the ideal of justice. This consideration raises two important questions. First, to what extent, and in what ways, is our capacity to define and institute justice limited and frustrated by external conditions? Second, when justice is limited in this way, must the ideal be adapted to the limiting external conditions, or must those conditions be challenged by the demands of justice?

In this essay, I am particularly concerned with two conditions sometimes thought to be external in this sense: want and scarcity. I argue that scarcity is indeed external to justice's ideal, and that whether want is also external depends on how want is determined. Those wants we have under more just social arrangements should be consistent with justice because they are formed through relations framed by justice's ideal. This quality of want, I then try to show, bears on the condition of scarcity.

For most theorists, restricting justice to situations where scarcity does not apply would make justice irrelevant to the world we live in; indeed to any world we might possibly live in. If this is the case, it would seem better to find a concept of justice applicable where there is not enough wealth to satisfy wants. In other words, it makes more sense to adapt the concept of justice to the realities of the world than to judge the world against a standard that cannot be met. That a standard of want satisfaction cannot be met only follows, however, if scarcity is an unavoidable condition. Yet, scarcity can only be understood that way if it is a necessary state; and this is difficult to establish.[5] Scarcity may not be a necessary condition, but a social artifact resulting from the character of want as that develops on a specific and contingent basis. If this is the case, we need not adapt our concept of justice to the condition of scarcity, but can instead judge the condition of scarcity according to its conformity with the idea of justice. I will not, then, assume that the concept of justice should be defined under a regime of scarcity, although I do consider justice in relation to conditions where means limit want satisfaction.

I suggest above that limiting justice to fairness, dueness, equality, and so on, limits our understanding of the justice of social, and especially economic, arrangements. Yet, to sever any link between justice and equality, dueness, impartiality, or fairness, clearly leaves justice without much that we value in it. Dueness, fairness, and impartiality all entail a kind of equality, the kind associated with equal regard for personhood. What is unfair or arbitrary is likely to be unjust, as is receiving what is due another. Yet, how do we know what is fair, what we are due, or along which dimensions we ought to expect equal treatment? The answer presumably lies in the idea of justice itself. Defining justice as fairness, dueness, or equality, reverses the relation of justice to its elements. That is, we know what is fair or due by asking what is just; we do not determine what is just by referring to fairness or dueness. Yet, if this is to work, we must have a more general notion of justice that could subsume dueness, fairness, or equality as elements.

One way to arrive at a more general notion is to see what the different partial concepts have in common. This procedure is, of course, somewhat arbitrary, especially given the ad hoc way I introduced those partial concepts. Still, the procedure can help motivate a discussion that, while admittedly less than rigorous, might be of use to those interested in rethinking problems of justice and the economy.

If we ask what the various terms linked above to justice share, it is concern with respect for the differences between persons, and with determining which differences are appropriate and which are not. Unless we intend to move to the extreme of justice as sameness, even justice as equality must invoke difference to be meaningful. This is why the notion of equality runs into difficulty when used to define justice; it invokes difference while suggesting sameness. But, of course, if we are all the same, neither equality nor justice matter. Dueness, fairness, impartiality, and right all suggest ways of dealing with difference, and thus bring us somewhat closer to the heart of the matter. Each invokes a criterion for judging the appropriateness of differences in the treatment of persons.

Formulated in general terms, justice protects the boundaries between persons that allow them to be *different persons*. Justice thus incorporates the sameness and difference of a world of different persons. Injustice violates the boundaries between persons by making some the subjects of others, thus making them lesser persons, or even non-persons.

I am most concerned here with justice as an ideal embodied in institutions. Justice is not simply a matter of fairness or dueness or even of living with others, but of institutions designed to assure fairness or dueness or regard for others in areas where failing to do so is not simply lamentable but rectifiable.[6] To be rude is to treat others without due regard; but it is not unjust. To allocate praise or blame where it is undeserved is unfair, but not a matter for intervention by the institutions of justice. Justice has a narrower claim within the broad territory marked out by concerns of mutual regard, fairness, and dueness. This is the claim we associate with making what is right a matter of law, and with the social institutions mandated to right and secure the individual's capacity to exercise rights and respect their exercise by others.

Yet, to become real, the ideal of living with others must be more than a matter of law, or of right embodied in law; it must be a matter of the way people lead their lives, whether regulated by law and supported by government or not. If we cannot live with others, or do not really know what that means, institutions of justice cannot take root. Those institutions must be embedded. And, while the institutions of justice can advance the ideal of justice, they cannot make it real on their own. There must also be an attitude that sustains justice.

The attitude appropriate to justice entails regard for others; and the institutions of justice embody the ideal also embodied in that attitude. Regard for others unites identity and difference when we understand it as regard for the self in others.[7] Only then can justice develop as the defining attribute of institutions that embody the idea of regard for the self in others.

Self-interest

Self and other

My emphasis in the following, then, will be on justice as living with *others*. It may seem that treating justice as the way we live with others makes it synonymous with our social condition, but this is not the case. We can, and often do, live together (socially) without much recognition that we live with persons different, and in any meaningful sense separate, from ourselves. To live with others poses a specific task, and makes specific demands on us. These tasks and demands, it turns out, are also those of justice.[8]

Recent interest in difference has made the other problematic and prompted a more serious consideration of what it is that makes someone other to us.[9] The growing concern with self and other has its roots in an idea about social determination. This idea connects social determination to identification of the individual with one or more social groups. Understood in this way, who we are depends on the groups to which we belong, groups based on race, ethnicity, gender, and so on. The social construction each group carries then becomes the social construction of the member.

Group identification significantly affects the way the individual is recognized by others. Indeed, group identification can eclipse individual identity.[10] To share a group membership is to share a group identity, and to that extent a sense of self. Those who do not share that identity are others to us as we are to them.

The boundaries of the group, and therefore of its individual members, must be made real, and this can only be done if the difference between member and non-member has salience. This is the salience of exclusion. Being excluded must matter. Because exclusion matters, being other also matters. Out of this construction, powerful claims have emerged about the idea of the other, advanced most prominently in the context of gender differences, but also extending to other important group identifications. These claims have to do with the way self uses other. Here, the other is not merely different. Rather, self and other also take on the significance of subject and object. The other as object is also a receptacle for disavowed parts of the self, and is treated in accordance with that role, a role that is imposed on, or otherwise adopted by, those who in society are given the status of not-self (or less than self).

Because of the complex implications of group identification for the differences between persons, self and other, especially considered as a unit, cannot be taken for granted, and I will not do so here. At the same time, I will not place so great an emphasis on group identification, nor will I treat self and other as inherently group phenomena. While I do consider groups, especially nations, and thus group identifications, my primary concern is with the separation between persons, and the relation of self to other in the context of this separation.

By proceeding in this way, I do not intend to suggest that matters of group identification, and self-other relations developed in the group context, are unimportant, or even less important. In the context of justice, it is also important, however, to consider self and other as interpersonal and intrapsychic phenomena, which is how I will treat them here. As I try to emphasize, this does not mean abandoning the idea of social determination, although it may mean altering somewhat how we understand that idea.

The separation of persons

The prominence of issues about groups having to do with exclusion of non-members and the use of the other means it is no longer as easy as it once was to take for granted the separation between persons that creates self and other. But, it is not only concern for issues of group identification that challenges us to consider more systematically the idea of self and other. A change in our understanding of psychic structure also leads in that direction. In particular, the idea that intrapsychic life has a social determination has significant implications for the way we understand the separation between selves.

If we do not take that separation for granted, for example as a physical attribute or natural condition, then we must see it as an attainment. As an attainment, it has certain conditions, in this case of a social character.[11] Where these conditions have been met, separation of persons is a possibility. So far as this separation is important to justice, including economic justice, realizing the social pre-conditions for the separation of persons is also important to achieving justice. We are not all separate persons; and we do not all experience a world of others to whom we might relate. Problems arise for many in recognizing the self-boundaries that constitute others for them.[12]

If the question about justice is what does it mean to live with others, a prior question must be: what makes a person someone other than ourselves? Although it may seem trivial, the answer must be that what makes someone other than ourselves is that he or she is, indeed, an other, separate, and therefore different, self. To speak this way, of course, treats the self as something in its own right. This something is a structure of mind, or specific organization of mental life.

The practice of using the term self in this way has recently become more common, although the idea of the self employed in this practice has a long history.[13] We might say, then, that the idea is less new than the language in which we express it. Yet, changes in usage suggest changes in the idea, particularly emergence of dimensions previously hidden, poorly understood, or poorly developed. The change in usage to which I refer expresses a weakening of conviction about the (historical and empirical) inevitability of self-awareness and self-boundaries (both physical and psychic). Thus, for example, we know that perception of its physical boundaries depends on the self's maturation within a specific context of interaction. Without that context, even this quality of the self, often taken to be innate, can fail to develop. If it does fail, self-awareness may not be achieved, or not fully achieved. Considerations such as this warn us against taking self-awareness, and thus the self, for granted. This poses problems for the idea that it is the person, understood as a socially constructed and recognized entity, that is problematic, while the self, understood as a natural endowment is not.[14]

We accept that personhood has a social character because it refers to recognition by others of a socially defined position or set of positions. The social character of personhood, then, means placing the individual into a concrete social context. Using this notion of social determination, which equates it with contextualizing or situating, makes us doubt the social determination of the self, which appears as the individual's inner capacity to find a place, that is, to find his or her social determination.

Yet, if that capacity is not simply innate, but the result of a specific development (making use of an innate potential), which only comes about within a determinate context of interaction (especially of recognition) by others, then self-recognition, which follows from recognition by others, and thus the self, cannot be presupposed. Nor, since self-recognition is the precondition for the discovery of place in a concrete social context, can we separate being a person from being a self.

Then, it is not only the 'category of the person' that develops historically, but the self as well. Indeed, this development of the self as a structure and construct provides the concept of the individual with its underlying meaning and significance. What is unique about the differences that mark out individuals is their origin not in arbitrary natural contingency, but in the self. That is, to be an individual is not simply to be one member of a class (thus to be particular yet undifferentiated) nor simply to be arbitrarily different from other members of that class, but to develop differences expressive of an internal structure we call a self. These are, then, self-determined differences

If being a person means, among other things, being a 'subject of intrinsic purpose' (Taylor 1985, p.260), the intrinsic quality of the purpose lies in its connection to the self; what is intrinsic is the self. Heinz Kohut (1977) uses self in this way, to refer to what he terms a 'center of initiative in the world'. Speaking this way connects the self to notions of acting and willing. The difference lies primarily in the way more recent thinking makes the capacity for acting and willing problematic. We cannot assume that members of society have this capacity, and that any impairment in willing stems from external constraints or irrational impulse. Something more is needed.

This something more is the forming of a mental structure appropriate to the task of being a self in the world: being autonomous, being aware of self-boundaries, knowing the self (its wants, capacities, and ends). The term mental, or psychic, structure refers to a complex of ideas, to the feelings attached to those ideas, and to an agency of the mind that judges actions of self and other, mobilizing feelings (such as guilt or pleasure) in the service of judgment (see Ogden 1986). This complex structure can either inhibit or facilitate action that realizes or expresses attributes of the self. The complex of ideas frames a self-idea, which establishes the extent to which we think of ourselves as centers of initiative rather than, for example, the objects of fate (see Bollas 1989).[15]

Many ideas people have about themselves, ideas such as inadequacy or incompetence, inferiority or subordination, impede initiative and impair the self.[16] Thinking about ourselves in these ways limits the extent to which what we do expresses our selfhood, and the extent to which it makes sense for us to act on our own initiative, or even to have any real initiative of our own.[17] Not only do these ideas impair our selfhood, however, they also invite the intrusion of others. That is, they imply weakened self-boundaries, and therefore make us vulnerable to others. To be inadequate or incompetent, or to relate to the world as though you are, implies that you need others to accomplish, and possibly even define, your ends. To be inferior or subordinate means to be determined by others, that is other selves.

The relations with others that emerge out of these self-ideas are not relations of self and other, but relations through which we borrow other selves, or have them imposed on us, while our own self is denied and undermined. Within these relations, separation of persons is not fully accomplished since we do not find different selves, and therefore a self relating to others.[18] In these respects, the organization of psychic life has much to do with the possibility of being a self; and the forces responsible for shaping mental life are also responsible for determining whether we develop, and live our life in accordance with, that internal agency we refer to as a self. Forming an appropriate internal structure involves integration of a unit self, which is an end and not a presupposition.

Justice institutes the idea of a bounded self. The bounded self depends on the achievement of what has been termed unit status (see Winnicott 1988). While the potential to develop the unit status that marks a bounded self may be innate, the actual development of that status depends on the interpersonal and institutional milieu. In this sense, the notion of a bounded self incorporates a notion of its social determination. The attribute of its milieu most profoundly implicated in the success or failure of this development of the self is security. Indeed, the boundaries of the self only really exist when they can be secured; and, in this sense, the self and its interests only really develop in what has been termed an 'atmosphere of safety'.[19] Justice and its institutions are, then, very much concerned with security.

The security of the self, like the very organization of the self, is a matter of its social being and social determination. Many students equate the social determination of the self with its embedding in a specific cultural context. Here, I explore the implications of treating selfhood as a social condition, not because it is socially contextualized in the sense currently popular, but because the unit status of the self only develops and thrives within a determinate set of social institutions and interactions: those appropriate to its security. These are institutions and interactions in which justice is intimately involved. In this sense, I treat the social determination of the self, or social self-determination, without the attendant presumption of a predetermined context given, for example, historically or culturally.[20]

Organizing mental life into something we can refer to as a self is neither automatic nor inevitable.[21] Some would even question whether it is possible or desirable. Be that as it may, the idea of justice involves a way of thinking about social institutions that leads toward a notion of the self as a structure. At least, it does so when we make the link between justice and living with others explicit. Then, justice gets wrapped up with the idea of a self, and the related ideas of self-interest and self-determination. Those ideas entail achieving a goal, difficult to attain, often only partly reached, sometimes rejected as undesirable or impossible. Whether the separation of persons that constitutes self and other will be achieved depends on the self's interpersonal world, and on the larger milieu of social institutions. That larger milieu can impede development of the separateness of persons in order to subordinate members to group identification and group solidarity.

Of course, as members of groups, we can relate to non-members as others. Yet, there is always an important sense in which these others are not other selves. The group dynamic tends to challenge any idea that the other is also the same, at least in the space of the self. Thus those who are other because they are not members of our group are either non-selves or lesser selves. In relating to them we are not relating to others in the sense I use that term here, of other selves.

Only to the extent that persons are separate units, and this cannot be assumed but needs to be established, must they relate to others.[22] Solving the problem of relating to or recognizing others is an important part of what we mean by maturation. We do not begin life with a developed sense of self capable of defining boundaries and holding its ground in a milieu of others. In place of an internal self, the infant and young child substitutes the relation with the parent. In the medium of its relation with the parent, the infant borrows the self of the parent to assure its own reality in the world. This borrowing of the self of the parent establishes a dyad rather than two separate units.[23] The rule is merger rather than separation, one rather than self and other. Once (or perhaps if) the child develops a sense of his or her own self, borrowing from and dependence on merger with the parent will no longer be necessary. The key to this development is the formation of the child's capacity to recognize others, to make his or her world a world of many and not just two who are in fundamental ways only one.

A world in which we live in merged units is a world of corporate selves rather than relations of self to other.[24] Triadic and multiple relations can only arise for a self mature enough to find selfhood in others. For a dependent personality, others are not recognized as the objects of potential relations, but of merger into units. This means that the world is, or must be made into, a world of merged personhood. This is the world of good (merged into a unit) and bad (excluded from the unit).[25]

Once we gain the unit status needed to live in the world as a person with our own capacities and interests, we need no longer equate connection with merger, or seek to make our world exclusively one of corporate units. Instead, a new goal emerges: relating to others. In our relations with others, good and bad, understood in the sense just introduced, give way to right and wrong. Right and wrong structure a way of relating that recognizes the separateness of persons. While the judgment of good and bad in a relationship has to do with the satisfaction it affords, and the unit it creates, the judgment of right and wrong has to do with the recognition of self and other it sustains. They are, then, part of the language of justice.

Making the economy a part of the system of justice understood in this way subjects it to the principle of separation of persons and respect for others. In the following exploration of justice and the economy, I treat the principles of separation and merger as potentially but not inevitably conflicting. That is, they can rest more or less comfortably in their separate spheres; but they can also each lay claim to wider ground. Historically, the problem of justice has been one of finding and defending its territory against incursions by the principle of merger into the group. Yet, with the triumph of democracy and market economy, the problem also arises that the principle of separation may claim too much, as it does, for example, when we try to reduce familial relations to contract, or otherwise treat family members instrumentally. The central issue of justice and the economy is setting the limits of the sphere of justice, and within the system of justice, the limits of the economy.

Community

I suggest above that good and right refer to two aspects or moments of social being and social life. Let me put this point more directly. The first (good) grounds the process that binds members together into a group with a shared way of life. The second (right) grounds the process that protects difference within community. While the two aspects need not break apart or stand opposed, they often do, particularly for cultures strongly imbued with the goal of establishing the subordination of member to group. When the two moments separate, justice cannot both integrate community and protect difference.

Thus far, I have not explicitly emphasized the part played by justice in integrating community. Even those communities that go furthest in defining the member by his or her position in the group, and thus leave least room for individual differences rooted in the self, must deal with the problem of living with other selves.[26] Community takes the member beyond the primitive dyad, the two who strive to be one, to incorporate many and thus, to whatever primitive degree, others. Even for communities devoted to suppressing difference, living with others poses a challenge that must be met for the survival of the whole. Justice, therefore, has a place.[27]

Nonetheless, many communities seek to place others outside. For such communities, justice can only to a limited degree be an internal ordering principle, since difference is not developed within the community. Justice only fully enters community ideals when others are part of the community, so the relation to others is in that sense internal. Understanding the problem of justice as living with others need not entail reconciling externally determined differences (i.e. external to life with others). Much depends on what we mean by other and difference.

To the degree that communities impede development of individuality, they do not develop the ideas of self and other.[28] Striving for merger, sameness, oneness, they strive to dispel any confrontation with others, and therefore any issue pertaining to justice as a principle ordering the inner life of the community. Within such communities, living with others is not a problem (or is suppressed as a problem) since others are not acknowledged (allowed to exist). Or, so far as it becomes a problem, it challenges the basic nature of the community. Then, justice rebukes community.

When we say that justice is how we live with others, we take others into community. When we recognize others as also part of our community, we recognize them as, in that sense, the same as ourselves. The problem of justice is one of finding sameness in difference. This means that what resides within also resides outside, within others, and yet does so in a way that not only preserves their difference from us, but actually constitutes that difference. We use the term self to refer to this unifying force that exists both within and outside, whose existence is the root both of the sameness and difference of persons. The problem of finding sameness and difference is the problem of defining the self as a unit; it is, therefore, the problem of self-determination, which is the defining concern of justice.

Yet, while self-determination is the defining concern of justice, it is also what makes justice problematic. When we take self-determination to mean pursuit of self-interest, and self-interest to mean disregard for others, it can lead away from justice. Much depends on how we interpret the self and its interests.

The problem of justice is sometimes formulated as the problem of dealing with conflict of interests.[29] The separation of persons means the separation of interests, which become particular to particular persons. This does not make interest all particular, or override the universal aspect of the self and its interest. Making interests particular and different does, however, follow from the separation of persons. In economics, and to a degree in other disciplines, interests are assumed to be determined prior to, and outside of, relations between persons, which are understood as instrumental to interests.[30] Because they are preformed in this sense, interests will only by accident lead to relations that embody the ideals we associate with justice. That is, persons pursuing their interests might act in ways that incorporate regard for others, but they might not. When they do not, the interests of persons and the ends of justice diverge.

Regard for others should not be taken to mean placing the interests of others, or of community, above those of the self. We can treat others with due regard while using them to achieve our own ends. We use others to attain our ends without violating their personhood when that use is reciprocal. This reciprocity, in which each attains his or her ends in a relation with another, sustains regard for others without giving up self-interest. Because exchange is, at least in principle, a relation of reciprocity, the market has special relevance in linking regard for others with pursuit of self-interest.

If, however, the interests justice deals with do not incorporate the ends justice incorporates, those interests cannot be assumed to make living with others possible. For some, this implies that conflict of interests must be resolved by force. Use of force, in effect, attacks the difference between self and other. The familiar equation of right with power acknowledges the irreconcilability of interests formed in ways that fail to incorporate regard for others, and thus of the separateness of persons that we have in mind by justice.

When we can use others to accomplish our ends, and gaining their consent has benefits for us, justice turns away from power. It turns toward the reciprocal use persons make of each other when force satisfies no one's interests well. To the extent that the instrumental orientation toward others respects their separate existence as persons in their own right, it can be just, and indeed, the justice of economic arrangements incorporates this attitude.

What remains to be explored is what about interests makes reciprocity better than force. Is it that use of force elicits a response less beneficial than use of positive incentives? Or, is it that use of force constitutes a relation that denies personhood at both poles, and thus is not an effective instrument of interest even for those with superior means? Use of force loses its effectiveness to the degree that interest has preservation of a (separate) other in a relation as its goal. An interest of this kind incorporates the main concern of justice.

Before considering further the problem of justice and self-interest, it may be helpful to explore what we have in mind by the terms interest and self-interest. The term interest refers to an attitude toward objects, both internal and external. We have an interest in objects that have significance for us because they are bound up in some way with who we are, and therefore with the gratification of our selves.[31] Then, to explore social being without a notion of interest is to explore it without a concept of self. Because justice is so much bound up with self and other, it must also be bound up with the matter of interest, especially with what interests the self.

Interest connects persons with various kinds of objects: things, ideas, institutions, groups, other persons, and themselves. That interest connotes connection does not imply that the source of interest is exclusively within the individual considered without regard for his or her social condition and social determination. It does not commit us to any method that entails reduction of the social to the individual. As a starting point, it does no more than focus our attention on the idea of a motivation to achieve a connection that has meaning and significance.

To say that we are motivated to pursue our interests leads to the question: In what do persons take an interest? At first glance the answer to this question will seem impossibly diverse and concrete. How could we begin to imagine a single object of interest, not only for a given individual, but for the multitude of real and possible individuals about whom our question might be asked?

It has been the habit in economics, and lately in other social sciences, to assume that this question is amenable to a simple response, that there is, indeed, one thing in which we have an interest, one object that motivates us in life: our selves. As an assumption, however, self-interest leaves much to be desired since it is not clear in what the object of self-interest (the self) consists. Still, on matters of justice and the economy, self-interest has special importance, since both economy and justice institutionalize its pursuit.

In the following, I treat self-interest as an interest in being a (particular) self, and in making that self real in the world. The quality of the self that combines particularity with reality in the world is *identity* (see Erikson 1956 and von Broembsen 1989).[32] To be a self is to be self-identical, that is to have continuity across time. To have an identity, then, is an important part of what it means to be a particular person. Only through particularity is personhood made real. To lack an identity is not to be a person.[33]

As I suggest above, a vital element of identity is the idea (conscious and unconscious) we have of who we are and hope to be. To have an identity means, then, to have an ideal of the self or ego ideal.[34] Our interest is in finding our ideal self and making it real, or in realizing the idea we have about ourselves in the world, especially in relation to others.

The mainspring of interest in the effort to shape at least a part of our world according to the idea we have about ourselves has special relevance to the individual and his or her interests. But, it can also apply to institutions and especially to the overarching public institution, the state, with its unique public interest.[35] The state can also have an idea about its world and act to make its world conform so far as possible with that idea. Thus, both public and private interest originate in ideas about the world, and about the place of the subject (individual or state) in that world.

The term self-interest, then, means an interest in a way of being in relation to others. For this way of being to define a self, however, it must be one among many. That is, to be a self, the person must establish unit status. To have a bounded self, to be one, involves knowing limits. Knowing limits is essential to participation in a system of justice, which, at its core, is a system that establishes and protects the integrity of the unit.

Self-interest, then, has two aspects, one internal, one external. Internally, to be a self is to establish secure self-boundaries, to know what is internal (self), and what is not (other). We refer to this aspect of self-interest when we speak of knowing yourself. Externally, to be a self means to make your self real in the world, especially the world of other selves. We refer to this aspect of self-interest when we speak of expressing and realizing the self. Both aspects of self-interest are important concerns of justice.

The key to having secure self-boundaries is living in a world that respects limits, where violation of the domain of the self is not the norm. Repeated violation of self-boundaries, whether physical or psychological, fosters insecurity, and undermines the development of the unit status that comes with a clear understanding of where 'I' ends and 'other' begins. Because of this, insecurity entails not only a failure to integrate the self, but also the parallel failure to appreciate, and thus respect, the selfhood of others.

This connection between security, integration, and respect for boundaries between self and other is a fundamental concern of justice, which is the way we live with others. Without security, there can be no life with others, since there can be no real respect for the boundaries that constitute self and other. Put the other way around, justice must mean security for the unit status of the self. As a matter of the configuration of institutions and regulation of relations between persons, a just society assures, so far as possible, security of the member's self.

The connection of justice to security can hardly be overemphasized today, when many assume that security undermines initiative and endangers efficiency allowing the lazy and ineffective unfairly to acquire the product of the inventive and industrious. Justice, with its mandate to make the self secure, challenges any argument favoring insecurity. If the argument linking efficiency to insecurity holds, then justice challenges efficiency. In the next Chapter, I consider the problematic relation between justice and efficiency.

Security does not mean that social institutions assure want satisfaction without regard to individual willing and acting, as critics of welfare measures and the welfare state often insist. They, of course, see an inherent conflict between security assured by institutions, and individual autonomy. Clearly, to provide for want satisfaction without regard to individual willing and acting violates the prerogatives of the self, as much conservative social policy rhetoric insists when it denounces the paternalism of government in the area of social welfare. That same rhetoric, however, assumes that self-interest can be taken for granted, or formed in a crucible of insecurity and an endangered self, that the self can know and act on its interests when its boundaries are not secure, and its very survival at stake.

This assumption conflicts with the idea that self-interest involves security of self-boundaries formed and maintained in the interaction of self and other. The interest justice has in security of the self can encompass not only those rights favored by conservatives, such as the right to own and use property, but also other rights rooted in the need to protect the self, including possibly a right to something we might call subsistence, a concept I will explore at greater length further on.

The central concern of the self is its unit status (the internal aspect), and the central problem of the self is to make that unit status real in the world (the external aspect). Making its unit status real means making the subjective objective. Objectivity for the self means that it exists outside. Other selves confront the individual with selfhood in an objective, that is external, form. Because of this, some emphasize recognition by others as the medium for making the self real.[36]

Recognition poses a problem. Recognition by others unites sameness and difference. As selves, we are the same, and can recognize our common personhood. As separate selves, we are different, and can gain recognition for our particularity. Yet, particularity must be the particularity of a self for its recognition to bring recognition of selfhood. Put another way, we seek to be a particular instantiation of self. If this works, recognition will be central to matters of justice, since it confirms self-boundaries, and thus the reality of self and other. But, it may not work. One or the other pole, of sameness or difference, may break off.

Recognition of sameness without adequate difference means merger into a single unit where self-boundaries are porous or non-existent. This erosion of self-boundaries erodes the relation between self and other, which is the defining concern of justice. Recognition of difference without sameness means indifference to others, which obstructs recognition of selfhood in the other. This makes mutual regard problematic, since mutual regard implies need for, rather than indifference to, the other. If we take seriously this need for the self to find itself outside, we can ground the idea of recognition in a fundamental interest of the self. Doing so, as I suggest below, has implications for justice.

It is not, however, only relations with others that establish the reality of the self. The world of things can also be, in its way, a world of selfhood. Things take on meaning in a world of persons who own, use, and produce them. Things produced for use embody a meaning that can only be realized in their relation to persons. Ownership of things becomes something real through recognition of the owner as a property owning person capable of embodying self into object. Because of this, it is not only in the world of others, but also in the world of things that we can find ourselves. The idea that property entails an attachment of thing to self carries this significance.

Traditionally, security of the self means respect for property right. This connection leads to the frequent equation of economic right with property right, and security with protection of that right. The implication is that protection of the unit status of the self comes with making property and person inviolate. It remains to be considered, however, what conditions must be met if property and person are to be secure. In particular, legal protection of property right may not be sufficient to secure the institution of property, and the unit status of the self bound up with it. These considerations turn out to be important for justice because of its connection to the idea of a unit subject seeking to make itself objective in its relations to others and to things. This is the interest of the self, and understood in this way, self-interest leads to a seeking after others.

Justice cannot, then, be rooted in altruism or self-denial, but only in our capacity to recognize and respect the self in others. Charity does not achieve the ends of justice. Yet, the capacity to respect the selves existing outside us stems from the respect we have for the self inside. Both are instances of respect for selfhood, an idea and attitude responsible both for self respect and respect for others.[37] Thus, the nature of our interest in others has the same ground as the nature of our interest in ourselves. We treat others with due regard for their personhood because we bring to our relations with and attitude toward others a reasonably secure sense of ourselves.[38]

This is obvious if we bear in mind that respect for ourselves and respect for the self in others both depend on our ability to recognize selfhood and respect its unit status, to know its boundaries whether they be our own or those of others. This respect for boundaries is the essence of any system of justice organized around rights, including the right to own property, which, of course, has special importance in political economy.

If the capacity to treat others with respect depends on the respect we have for ourselves, then justice requires that individuals establish and maintain a reasonable self-feeling. This implies that self-interest, rather than opposing justice, is one of its most important foundations. A system of justice must, then, include adequate space for the self to emerge and pursue its interests. This space is the milieu for pursuit of self-interest Hegel refers to as 'civil society'. The modern economy is an institution within civil society. It plays a vital role in organizing society's economic life to assure that the individual has the opportunity to find him or her self in the world, and to make a part of the world accord with the self. The question of the just economy has to do with the shape of economic institutions required to secure this opportunity for the self.

The relationship between justice and security emphasized here clarifies the idea that the real needs of the self are those it would have if subject to its own determination. This idea is not unfamiliar since it means that self-interest emerges for a self that is *free*. The connection of self-interest to freedom usually carries the implication that external coercion must be removed for the self to pursue its interests. Justice, then, protects the self from such coercion, and thus is linked through freedom to self-determination.

Preventing external coercion secures the space of the self and allows for self-action. Put this way, the link between justice and security is a familiar one. The question remains, however, whether preventing coercion is enough to secure the self. Those who advocate minimal government sometimes think this way, and, as I suggest above, treat any other mandate of government as an intrusion that, far from securing the self, violates and even enfeebles it.

Clearly we gain little benefit if government protects us from the violence of others only to perpetrate violence of its own. Further, self-determination can hardly mean the kind of dependence that diminishes the self, whether that dependence is on others or on government. What is missing in advancing this judgment is the distinction between situations where the self is internally secure enough to determine itself and pursue its interests, and situations where it is not. We can avoid this distinction by assuming that the only impediments to self-determination are external, so that freeing the self from external coercion literally means freeing it for its own determination. But, this might not be true. If it is not, a system of justice concerned only with removing obstacles fails to assure provision of the conditions necessary for justice, which include conditions needed to make the removal of obstacles the path to self-determination. This indicates why, as I suggest above, providing legal protection for property may not secure the institution of property.

Public and private interest

Interest in self and other

I suggest above that many students find a unity in the apparent diversity of interests by seeing all interest as interest in the self. Since the end of the Nineteenth Century, economists have taken this notion of unity a step further by making all self-interest an interest in a single self-feeling, variously termed happiness, pleasure, and satisfaction. Thus, the individual's end is to attain a (positive) feeling, and to attain as much of that feeling as possible. If we accept this way of thinking about want and interest, then individuals do indeed have only one interest, although it may be attained in different ways, especially for different persons.[39]

Some typical implications of this idea can be found in the standard treatment of what economists refer to as 'public goods'. The theory of public goods offers an apparently clear and simple way of distinguishing between public and private on the basis of technical attributes of goods. Goods are private if others can be excluded from their consumption; they are public if such exclusion is technically impossible.

If exclusion is not possible, then many who gain satisfaction from consumption of the public good need not pay any of its cost. Even though the benefits to the aggregate of consumers exceed total production cost, and thus satisfaction is enhanced overall by their provision, public goods will not be privately produced, since any potential private producer must bear the whole cost while appropriating only a small part of the benefit. In general, then, cost for the producer will exceed benefit. This means that government can increase the overall level of satisfaction by providing the good, and financing it through taxes that distribute cost among those who stand to benefit.

Public goods, understood in this way, imply no distinction between private and public wants or interests, but only between classes of goods all destined to satisfy private want. The public goods theory assumes, in other words, that persons have only one kind of want: the desire for self-satisfaction. The absence of a distinction between classes of interest unifies the concerns of economics and politics by making politics the pursuit of private ends by other than market means. Public goods define one instance where market means will not best satisfy private ends.

Some argue against the idea that interests are of one kind (see Taylor 1982 and Anderson 1990). If they are correct, then we can also use interests to distinguish public from private. Such a distinction would, of course, be more fundamental than that centering on technical attributes of objects. Such technical attributes of objects might remain relevant, but only understood in the context of a theory of interests or ends. But, how can we know whether interests are, indeed, singular or multiple?

The idea that the force of the self unifies interests is a powerful one. At the same time, the notion that interests are of different kinds helps us take into account the complexity of human motivation, and the possibility that being a self does not exclude pursuit of ends of different kinds. The opposition between the two assumptions, that interests are ultimately of one kind (for one thing) and that they are multiple, places us in a dilemma, since neither option taken by itself proves altogether satisfying.

While interests may be classified in various ways, the dilemma just introduced arises primarily because of the classification of interests into those we have when acting for ourselves and those we have when acting for others. The problem is to determine if these are, indeed, interests with different origins and opposed ends, or if they are in some sense pointed in the same direction.

Finding unity becomes difficult when we assume that one class of interests implicates the self in a positive way, the other only negatively. If acting for others means acting against the self, our interest in ourselves cannot lead us to act for others. Then, if we are to act for others, which might include acting in the public interest somehow defined, we will be acting on interests not our own. Since the resources we use in doing so could also be used in our own interest, acting for others implies acting at the expense of the self. There is in this an implied repression of self of the kind, for example, sometimes associated with duty. Our interests in self and other must, then, have fundamentally different origins.[40]

Economists sometimes avoid this result by assuming we never act for others, but only seem to do so. Helping others is not something we do for them, but something we do for ourselves, for the satisfaction doing so provides us. What appears as acting for others actually serves our own ends because we do it to gain the same satisfaction, happiness, or pleasure we pursue when acting more obviously for ourselves. This makes altruism an instance of self-interest. It is not, then, a matter of following duty against the self, but of gaining the same satisfaction sought when acting in more recognizably self-interested ways.

We will only integrate unity and diversity of interest if we give up the assumption that acting for others is the same as acting for ourselves without then assuming that acting for others means acting against the self. Acting for others might not be acting either for or against our selves if it means acting out of regard for the self in others. If acting for others means acting with regard for the self in others, it has the same root as acting for self. The difference lies in whether the object of our action (the self) is taken in its particular aspect as *our* self, or in its universal aspect as the self existent both within us and others.[41]

Because our interest in the self includes an interest in the self in others, self-interest means an interest in others. This can be an interest in other particular selves, in which case we refer to it as regard for others. Regard for others has special importance to justice, including economic justice. But, regard for others is also an instance of the more general regard for self that forms the mainspring of all our interest. The problem with the economist's way of thinking referred to above is not so much that it only allows for one kind of interest, but that the interest it allows for is all particular. The economist's way of thinking does not connect an interest in a particular self with an interest in selfhood as such. It does not, then, consider the qualities all particular selves share, qualities that make particular selves particular ways of being a self.

Regard for the self goes beyond other particular selves when it becomes regard for selfhood as such. This regard for self provides an important root for a (public) interest of the group as the steward of a self-ideal only partially realized in the lives of its individual members, and on which the particular self-ideals depend. The group self-ideal is the universal that exists in and through the members' particular selves. This object of the public interest is, however, also the object of the self-interest of the individual, whose interest in his or her self would mean very little if it were not simultaneously a more general interest in what it means to be a self.

Dependence of our particular self-interest on a more general interest in selfhood follows from the connection between being a self and gaining recognition. If we assume that being a self does not depend on recognition of our selfhood by others, then we also assume that being a self is a purely personal and internal matter. But, if we assume that a self we cannot in principle make intelligible to others is not a self, then we cannot be a self without incorporating the universal ideals and meanings of selfhood that make what we are an instance of being a self.

While establishing a universal self-ideal has vital importance to the individual's project of being a self in the world, it is also possible that our concern with the universal will lead us to lose sight of the particular. When, for example, we fail to take into account individuality and autonomy in providing for wants, the particular moment of self-interest gets put aside. Thus, welfare systems that foster dependence, either on private charity or the state, incorporate a concern for others that falls short of a concern for their particularity, and thus for the self in other. Many critics of the welfare state grasp this point, if in a one-sided way. They understand how little welfare systems concern themselves with the particular aspect of the self and, by failing to nurture that dimension, fail to revive the person's inner capacity for self-directed action and initiative.

Being a self demands the opposition of, and the limits set by, the world of others and by the ideal of selfhood that exists in different particular forms. This presence of self simultaneously as universal and particular is what we mean by its social determination. Because of this social determination of the self, it must be both for itself and for others, which implies a unity in difference of self-interest.

Political economy and self-interest

The history of political economy is in many ways a history of an idea about self-interest. This is the idea that the social order is, or could be, a system of private persons each pursuing his or her unique particular interests. In political economy this becomes a system in which the universal aspect of self-interest just considered does not exist. Political economy, then, attempts to see each self-interest as a unique event rather than as an instance of the general phenomena of interest in the self. Because of this, political economy can only with difficulty imagine how our self-interest might lead us to take an interest in others, or in the community as a whole.

For the classical economists, each individual learns how attaining his or her ends depends on assisting others in attaining theirs. This is because each discovers that they will gain more of what they want if they specialize in a system of division of labor than if they attempt to be self-sufficient. The division of labor leads to a kind of concern for others, the kind that follows from the fact that we depend on others for some of what we need. Implicitly, we depend not simply on particular others, but on the system as a whole, the social division of labor, of which we are a part and not an isolated event. It could be said of this conception, as Hegel does, that it carries implicit in it the idea that self-interest is an interest in others. Since the idea is there, if only implicitly, the groundwork is set for its emergence in consciousness as an idea about social interdependence. During the classical period in political economy, this construction carries the burden of the notion that self has universal as well as particular aspects.

Because political economy after the classical period tends to eliminate any emphasis on a social division of labor or system of mutual dependence, this implicit idea of a universal aspect of self-interest falls even further from sight.[42] Political economy now attempts to conceive a system of individual selves whose uniqueness has reached a point where we can no longer say they are instantiations of a universal self-idea, and not simply unique events unto themselves.

The diminishing importance of the idea of a system of mutual dependence moves us toward a system in which selfhood is all particular, or at least attempts to be. This naturally makes any idea of a public interest irreducible to the particular interests of individuals impossible; thus, economists shy away from that idea. They have difficulty imagining public ends irreducible to pure particular interests.[43] Some simply insist that any notion of group ends other than the aggregate of predetermined individual interests must be metaphysical (Buchanan and Tullock 1962, chapter 1).

The public interest

By identifying the public interest with an interest in the self, we establish a foundation for linking public and private ends so that the two need not conflict (although they may under particular circumstances). Yet, the idea that the public interest is an interest in the self leaves open the question of the nature of the self that is the object of the public's interest.

This object of the public's interest might be the self as such, considered without the particular ends that distinguish individual personalities and ways of life. This universal self is what all persons have in common so far as they have developed a bounded self-identity with a reasonably secure sense of the self-other relation. It is instantiated in their particular ways of being a self.[44] If this self in general is the object of the public interest, then that object is justice as we have defined it here. Justice identifies and secures self-boundaries, assuring that each individual can be his or her own person. Beyond knowing and securing those boundaries, justice is not concerned with the specific content of self-ideals, or with the particular interests to which they lead. So long as those interests incorporate regard for the self in other, they are consistent with justice, and, on this definition, with the ends of the state, or the public interest.

Yet, the object of the public interest might also be particular, as would be the case if it incorporated ideals specific to particular nations or cultures. Then, the public interest would not simply be in the self as such, and therefore in justice, but in the more concrete content of the members' self-ideals. We speak of this aspect of the public interest when we argue for a public interest in raising the cultural level of citizens, preserving a common culture, or possibly maintaining a higher culture. This common, or possibly higher, culture embodies not simply what is just, but also what is deemed the good life within a specific context. The notion of the good, so far as it is not simply a matter of regard for the self in others, provides members with a group identity that sustains and constitutes their individual identities.

When the object of the public interest is the good in this sense, the citizens' self-ideas must incorporate a communal ideal, in however particular a form, if they are to establish the basis for a meaningful link to community, and thus see in the pursuit of public ends also the realization of their private interests.[45] The group self-idea, then, limits and determines the ideals of its members. If, however, the group attempts to make the latter immediately the same as the former, then the individual wants nothing but the welfare of the whole. If this is the case, there can be nothing to distinguish particular selves.

If the nation or community exists in a world of communities with different notions of the good life, this tends to sharpen the tension between the universal and particular in group self-ideals. Under these conditions, the group self-ideal, while universal for its members, may be particular when considered among its peers. Then, the community's self-idea is not simply the ideal of selfhood considered in general, outside of its particular forms as many particular, and thus partial, ways of life. It also takes on a special coloring that limits the ways we can be a self within our particular national culture.

In a world of different national cultures, claims for universality of cultural patterns within the nation run up against the reality of differences across nations that reveal that, what appears to be universal, is in fact partial. This can encourage an abstraction of the universal self-ideal away from any culturally specific content so that it may be consistent with diverse cultures. Thus, diversity of cultures undermines the claims each has over the individual, which is the original basis of diversity. Thus, diversity tends to undermine itself. In so doing, it sharply focuses the problem of understanding the nature of the universal self-ideal instantiated in a system of justice. In searching for a more general ideal, justice takes on special significance. The diversity of cultures, because it undermines the claims of each to universality, can encourage the development of the more general ideal of the self-determining individual, free to develop a sense of self and appropriate way of life within limits given only by the reciprocal freedom of all. In a world of national cultures, however, the universal is also, or at least seems to be, particular. This dilemma leads, on a practical level, to various solutions.

Celebrating cultural diversity both facilitates and undermines the effort to integrate a universal self-ideal. The more we focus on the particular, the more celebration of diversity erodes the security of the individual, who cannot be a particular person without the connection to the universal. We can only avoid this outcome by establishing a more universal group self-ideal that incorporates, but therefore also limits, diversity. The self-ideal linked to justice as living with others can play this role, although it can also corrode other group ideals so far as they conflict with regard for others.

Communities can lack sufficient integration of a collective self-ideal because they seek to embrace the diverse ideals of different cultures. Within such communities, the individual faces the dilemma that there is no self, there is only the plurality of selves. This situation makes selfhood problematic since, however the member attempts to become a self, he or she must fail. The issue of the connection of the particular ways of being a self to the universal self-ideal that defines the public interest is a vital one. It is at the center of the matter of the relation between the public and the private.

The public interest and the state

Talk of the public interest invokes a public subject: the whole, or the community, as subject. Thinking of the whole as subject poses the same problems we encounter when we attempt to treat the individual as subject. The individual is a subject only so far as he or she meets certain conditions that involve development of an integrated core or self, and the unit status associated with it. This core includes what we have referred to as a self-idea (or ego ideal). The self-idea guides action in the world.

Treating the whole as subject makes sense if the whole has an ideal appropriate to it, and can translate that ideal into plan and action. When this condition has been met, the whole becomes a subject. We can use the term state to refer to this whole constituted as subject (see Hegel 1956, pp. 73-9). But, if we are to think of the state as subject, we must separate out that aspect of the state, or that kind of state, to which this notion of subject can be applied. This requires that we make a distinction within our understanding of the state. This is a distinction between the action of a collective subject (state) and the activity of administering or executing laws derived from sources other than the state understood in this more limited sense. The distinction between the actions of a collective subject and the administrative duties of a public agency can mark out different theories of government and the state, or it can mark out different functions of government.

Following this second path, Hegel and Durkheim treat the true state as that part of government capable of defining its own ends.[46] They divide the state into two parts, one that thinks and decides, and another that administers. Because they see the true state as the collective subject, and not the administrative apparatus, they insist that the source of state action not be predominantly external, in interests arising in (civil) society, especially the economy. To the extent that external forces drive state action, it does not make sense to treat the state as the subject of its action.[47] How we resolve the question of the origin of state action has significant implications for how we understand the legitimacy of the state. I consider some of these implications in the next section.

More common than the interpretation offered by Hegel and Durkheim has been the idea that the true subject (so far as it is reasonable to speak in these terms) of public action is not the state, but the interests that influence the state apparatus. This idea has both positive and normative aspects. It accurately describes the (historical or empirical) state so far as the state has given up any mandate to act as collective subject, and has instead fallen under the dominance of (civil) society. Yet, this is possible in part because of the nature of the values instantiated in the state and its organization. That is, the state opens itself up to domination by civil society because the state makes private interest its normative end. A good example of this is the recent attack on government in the United States led in large measure by members of Congress in the name of democracy. Thus, the positive aspect needs to be considered in connection with the normative.

When the state joins the attack on the universal values and ends implicit in the particular private interests of citizens, the state can hardly then defend itself against pressure to give up its more universal mandate, and become the instrument of private interest. Once the state has become the instrument of private interest, the theory that understands it in that way and denies the significance of a distinct public interest becomes the dominant theory. Put more generally, abdication of the state's status as collective subject follows the subordination of the public to the private, and, in our terms, the subordination of the universal to the particular aspects of the self and its interests. As a practical matter, this sort of development is facilitated by the erosion of the ideal of a collective subject (or its failure to develop) .

The subordination of the universal to the particular and the reasons for it often adduced were articulated by Adam Smith in the last part of the Eighteenth Century (Smith 1937). Smith considered the state incapable of acting as a true public subject precisely because those who represent the state were, to his mind, incapable of rising above their own private and particular interests. Distrust of government follows from the assumption that it must, at least under all practically realizable circumstances, fall under the sway of private interests. Then, if public ends are to be achieved, they must be achieved otherwise than by public means. Thus, Smith invokes the invisible hand of the market to lead to the public good without calling on the knowing and willing of a collective subject.

The problem of the state

Smith's conclusion concerning the pursuit of public ends by private means retains its popularity. Those who attack the idea of the state as holder of a collective ideal often refer to the way the state is dominated by private interests. While Smith took this dominance to be a, perhaps lamentable, result of human nature, it can also be seen as a virtue, as it is by those who insist that the state incorporate a multiplicity of even competing group ends (see Dahl 1956). Then, the call for diversity as a virtue undermines the effort to establish the whole as subject, and to make the state capable of undertaking substantial projects in accord with a collective self-ideal.

These considerations can shed some light on the contemporary crisis of the state centering on its legitimacy as the bearer of a group ideal. The way of thinking about the state as collective subject only to a limited degree corresponds to the experience of the state common under a private enterprise economic system. Not only does it fail to mirror our experience of the state, however, it also conflicts with the ideal of the state dominant in market-centered economies. This failure in the realm of ideals has much to do with the state's failure on a practical level.

The dominant ideal of the state considers it the protector of private property, and gives the mandate to protect property to the state only because of limitations in the capacities of individual property owners to make their property secure. According to this interpretation, the state exists for instrumental reasons, and its real origin is in the pursuit of private ends. The idea that the state is no more than the facilitator of ends formed privately, without regard to the community, has led to the interpretation of the actual state as the object of private ends, rather than as the collective subject. The state appears more as a political system in the narrower sense of an arena for the clash of private interests than as the bearer of the public self-ideal and the group ends linked to it. This argument, because it overvalues the particular aspect of interest, tends to foster the ideal of a minimal state, with the implied tendency toward expansion of the private sector at the expense of the public.

Yet, even those who insist on a more substantial mandate for government may not effectively counter the argument against the state as collective subject. Thus, many who argue that the welfare of subordinate groups (for example women or ethnic and racial minorities), and the diverse cultures they represent, cannot be secured by the market, but must be part of a larger mandate for the state, often echo the emphasis placed on the particular by more conservative critics of government. They do so when their call to protect diversity is at the expense of the development within the state of a universal self-ideal. Diversity can develop out of a universal, and then provide the universal with a substantive content; or, it can displace the universal with incommensurable particular cultures and the self-ideals peculiar to them. In the struggle between these two configurations, justice hangs in the balance.

Since justice institutes a unit self and the self-other boundary consistent with it, justice requires that we understand the unity of self and other. Justice, then, institutes a universal self in and through a system of particular, individual, persons. If the state loses contact with the universal in favor of diverse particular cultures and associated selfhoods, it cannot sustain justice. The call to protect diversity can undermine development of a universal self-ideal that could make the state the collective subject. The extent to which it does so depends on whether protection of cultural diversity and subordinate groups displaces universal ideals that transcend the particularity of group cultures.

A parallel problem arises on the other side of the political spectrum. Conservative critics of the state still expect it to secure the institutions of a private enterprise market system, including the corporate organizations through which wealth is produced and circulated to those who will own and use it. On this side, the legitimacy of the state is important because the state has a vital function in assuring the well-being of a particular interest (of the business class) that is also universal in that it holds responsibility for group economic welfare.[48]

Yet, the legitimacy of the state cannot be secure under the dominance of particular interests and ideals, whether those are the interests and ideals of a business class or of subordinate and excluded groups. If we make protection of particular groups the end of the state, we undermine its legitimacy and therefore its ability to defend those groups. This is the problem the state encounters in the contemporary period.

The problem has been particularly acute in the area of economic policy. In economic policy, the movement for a balanced federal budget gains support from distrust of government. This distrust grows out of a feeling of insecurity on the part of citizens, and out of a sense that the government intends to serve not their interests, but the particular interest of favored groups (whether these be minorities or business or others perceived as partial interests). Yet, the implication of a balanced budget is significant weakening of the government's ability to cope with economic and social problems, problems ranging from business cycles and urban decay to securing the rights of individuals or the well-being of members of disadvantaged groups. The government's failure to deal with these problems further undermines its legitimacy. The proposed solution is, then, part of the problem.

When universal ends, such as protection of private property or securing the welfare of the disadvantaged, are advanced as particular ends of interest groups, they become particular ends, and, as such, lose much of their moral force. Yet, a political system that tends to transform all universals into particular interests undermines its own normative foundations. The resulting erosion of normative order places all particular interest at risk, since no particular interest can be achieved outside of an order carrying normative force.

More specifically, the attack on government weakens limits on the system of private property. While this attack intends to strengthen the private sector, in practice it tends toward the opposite result. By weakening the limits of private property, it also undermines the security of property. It does so, in part, because it undermines the legitimacy of the one institution capable of securing property right. When many do not have property, or property adequate to satisfy their needs, or when the property they have is not secure, then commitment to the system of property will not be strong.

The real solution to the problem of the state lies in tempering the connection of government to particular interest, but this demands that we conceive more than the particular in the interests of individuals and groups. Doing so has proven difficult for critics of government, whether they represent dominant or excluded interests. As a practical matter, moving toward a solution does not seem imminent. On a theoretical level, however, we can at least indicate a possible direction. In doing so, the idea of justice plays an important role precisely because it incorporates the universal implicit in particular interest. This universal is the ideal of self-determination.

The state committed to justice insists that it is equally true that without the universal self, there can be no selves, and without the particular selves, there can be no universal self. The diversity and particularity this state defends is that of autonomy or self-determination. Any other diversity is either derivative of self-determination, and thus protected with it, or a danger to self-determination, and thus something from which the individual deserves protection.

Notes

1 For these, see Walzer (1983), Miller (1976), Rawls (1971), Ginsberg (1965), and Nozick (1974).

2 The concept of income distribution, taken other than as a metaphor, can be misleading. Because of this, I will in the following more often refer to income difference than distribution thereby avoiding any commitment to the notion that there already exists something called income, which is then in some way distributed.

3 An exception to this would be for charges that inequalities of income and wealth derive from exploitation. I consider some of these in Chapter 2.

4 For a discussion and critique of this link see Zucker (1995).

5 The peculiarity of this assumption is indicated in Sahlins (1972, chapter 1).

6 This point is emphasized by Adam Smith (1969, pp. 157-60).

7 The unity of sameness (or identity) and difference is central to the problem of justice. For further discussion, see Desmond (1987, especially p. 5).

8 Thus, Adam Smith identifies injustice with doing harm to others, 'real and positive hurt to some particular persons' (1969, p. 157, see also p. 289). Smith has, as fits the context in which he wrote, a limited notion of what can be done to hurt others that falls into the class of injustice. The cases he suggests, especially murder and theft, indicate, however, the close link of justice to regard for the boundaries between self and other.

9 See Young (1990), Todorov (1993), and Yeatman (1994).

10 For illuminating examples see Schecter (1992); I explore the problem of individual and group identification in Levine (1996).

11 The relevant literature is surveyed in Greenberg and Mitchell (1983).

12 For a fuller discussion see Benjamin (1992) and Apprey and Stein (1993).

13 The earlier text most directly relevant to the usage favored here is Hegel (1977). In his sketch of an anthropological history of the self, Marcel Mauss (1985, p. 20) concludes that '[f]ar from existing as the primordial innate idea, clearly engraved since Adam in the innermost depths of our being, it continues here slowly, and almost right up to our own time, to build upon, to be made clearer and more specific, becoming identified with self-knowledge and the psychological consciousness'. Of special importance in more recent development of the idea is the work of Donald Winnicott and Heinz Kohut.

14 For an example of this idea, see LaFontaine (1985, p. 124).

15 In defining a person, Charles Taylor (1985) emphasizes 'self-interpretation', which is, in a sense, the active side of having a self-idea.

16 These ideas are complex structures in large part hidden from consciousness, and experienced in distorted and confusing ways. Changing ideas is no simple matter. Because the form in which we are aware of them distorts and hides their real qualities, we cannot simply decide to give them up. And, of course, being told by another to think, act, or believe differently, simply reproduces our problem, since the initiative remains outside. I do not here explore the way in which we develop these ideas, which is a process of the internalization of formative relations that become self-ideas. This process makes repression of the self, which begins as a matter of a relation with another, a matter of how we relate to ourselves. For a further discussion of these issues see Fairbairn (1952), Furman (1980), and Von Broembsen (1989).

17 Of course, the problem of initiative is a complex one, since transferring initiative to another also involves, and is in its way an expression of, our own initiative and therefore selfhood. This makes the use of language difficult, since we are compelled by the psychic and social reality to say that we are agents in the relation through which we lose our agency, and thus our selfhood. This complexity is explored in Schafer (1976) and Shapiro (1981)

18 This is also a matter of degree. When Winnicott speaks of achieving 'unit status' he has in mind something attained very early in life, which then establishes the basis for a subsequent personal development. Yet, it could also be said that the struggle for unit status and secure self-boundaries continues well into the more mature stages of development.

19 For discussion of this concept see Sandler (1987, Chapter 1) and Schafer (1983, Chapter 2).

20 For a critique of this assumption, see Winfield (1988c) and Maker (1994).

21 While it may be argued that even infants have a core of selfhood, it is still the case that the self as I consider it here, while arising out of that core, is not synonymous with it, but demands a special development; see Stern (1985).

22 This is a matter of degree, since only the most entangled dyad can even begin to approximate elimination of all separateness of persons. While, as a practical matter, we need to consider degrees of separation and merger, theoretically it is relevant to consider the idea of other selves as a qualitative rather than quantitative distinction.

23 This is the point forcefully brought to our attention by Donald Winnicott (1965); see also Ogden (1986, chapter 7).

24 It may be more precise to say this is a world where our psychic energies are devoted to the effort to overcome self-boundaries, and create corporate units often against the resistance of others.

25 This way of using the distinction between good and bad is adapted from Ronald Fairbairn's use of the terms good and bad object; see Fairbairn (1952).

26 See Lienhardt's interesting discussion of individual differences in African societies; Lienhardt (1985).

27 Even primitive communities take murder, the most immediate violation of the other, to be a crime; and even primitive communities have a sense of property, of what is connected to the particular personality (though this sense of property may seem distant from modern notions). Community does not mean elimination of self-boundaries, although some communities strive for that end; for examples, see Fitzgerald (1986).

28 For a fuller discussion see Chasseguet-Smirgel (1985).

29 For a fuller discussion of this way of thinking about justice see Barry (1989).

30 Thus, the most important normative condition in economics, Pareto Optimality, is defined on the basis of given preferences and endowments. For a critique of the idea that justice is based on presupposed interests, see Winfield (1988a and 1988b).

31 'If men are to interest themselves for anything, they must (so to speak) have part of their existence involved in it; find their individuality gratified by its attainment. ... Nothing therefore happens, nothing is accomplished, unless the individuals concerned, seek their own satisfaction in the issue' (Hegel 1956, pp. 22-3).

32 Throughout, I use the term particular to refer to those aspects that establish differences between selves. This usage is not inevitable since a particular member of a set may not be otherwise distinguished from other members (and therefore from the universal). It may be questioned, however, whether a member of a set not otherwise distinguished is truly particular. For a discussion see Winfield (1991, pp. 51-8).

33 'Clinical experience indicates that each person tries throughout life to cling to his own sense of self and identity and defends against whatever threatens his notion of who he is' (Volkan 1988, pp. 60-1). The idea of identity has important implications for the dialectic of self and other, particularly in the international and cross-cultural context.

34 For a discussion of the 'ego ideal' see Chasseguet-Smirgel (1985) and Sandler (1987, chapter 6); for a discussion of self-ideals in the

context of concerns closer to political economy, see Levine (1998).

35 Some theorists have difficulty with this. They find it metaphysical (if not mystical) to think that anything other than an individual could be a subject. These same thinkers, of course, have no difficulty with the assumption that the individual is a subject, taking this for granted, and thus failing to notice that it is no more or less metaphysical to assume that individuals are subjects than that the whole constitutes itself as subject (see Buchanan and Tulloch 1962).

36 The classic source is Hegel (1977, Part B). For more recent use of this idea see Benjamin (1992) and Winnicott (1974).

37 This idea is more fully developed by Jessica Benjamin (1992); see also Mitchell (1993, p. 34) and Ogden (1986, chapter 4).

38 For a fuller discussion, see Kohut (1977). Morris Ginsberg asserts that 'cognition of others does not necessarily imply respect for them as persons' (1965, p. 52), and, in noting this, seeks to discredit the view that self-consciousness entails any regard for self in other. This, I think goes too far in equating consciousness with cognition. To be conscious of another self means to be conscious of self-boundaries, which is exactly what it means to be conscious of self. The cognition of another as a physically separate unit does not, it is true, carry this implication. While others are physically separate units, otherness is not assured by physical separation and the cognition of it.

39 The idea that all interest is in some sense self-interest derives from the utilitarian roots of much current thinking in economics. If all motivation is ultimately the pursuit of pleasure and avoidance of pain, then this pursuit and avoidance is the substance of self interest, as the self is essentially the unit that feels pleasure and pain. This makes all ends ultimately one. From the beginning, however, economists have had their doubts. Thus, Jevons (1888, pp. 26-7) notes that '[m]otives and feelings are certainly of the same kind to the extent that we are able to weigh them against each other; but they are, nevertheless, almost incomparable in power and authority'. Jevons believes there are 'higher' and 'lower' pleasures, and that economics concerns itself with the latter. The idea of a ranking of ends within a larger utilitarian calculation is developed more recently by A.K. Sen (1977).

40 This is the position adopted for example by Adam Smith, who emphasizes the struggle of duty with self-feeling and the need to sacrifice private to public interest; see Smith (1969, pp. 232-60 and 384). Yet, Smith also emphasizes the pursuit of esteem in the eyes of others, a motivation that makes the interest in others an extension of self-interest and begins to bring in the notion of

recognition.

41 The problem of unity and opposition of the universal and particular is explored in Hegel (1977).

42 For a discussion of the absence of a notion of mutual dependence in modern economics see Levine (1977, chapter 6).

43 Indeed, starting with irreducibly particular interests poses intractable difficulties for the construction of any notion of a public interest, even the notion of a social preference ordering or community indifference curve. Arrow (1951) notes that we can construct a community preference ordering if individual preferences are not independent, but share certain characteristics, which they might if they are all particular versions of a universal.

44 The universal self considered here is similar to Benhabib's 'generalized other', although her way of distinguishing the generalized other from what she terms the 'concrete other' differs in important ways from the distinction here between universal and particular aspects of self; see Benhabib (1992, pp. 158-170).

45 This connection is often lost in treatments of the ego-ideal that restrict themselves to the particular side, which is common in psychoanalytic use of the term.

46 Durkheim (1958) goes so far as to exclude action altogether from the domain of the state which he considers the agency of collective thought. More recently, Stephen Krasner (1978) has attempted to identify the state with that part of government concerned with articulating ideological ends.

47 For a fuller discussion and survey of relevant literature, see Caporaso and Levine (1992, chapter 8).

48 This is the point emphasized in Lindblom (1977).

2 Economic justice

Work and pay

Work and consumption

If we think of the self-idea as a potential, we can understand the opportunity afforded by the economy as the opportunity to realize that potential as activity and product.[1] In economics, production is the process that realizes an idea (or plan) by using capacities to transform means into product. Production, then, embodies an idea or makes it objective.

We refer to the direct involvement of human beings in this process as 'work', a term with some complicated connotations.[2] The term work can be defined in purely physical terms (Marx does so when he introduces what he calls the 'labor process'). But, of course, work can have something peculiarly human about it, something lost when we think of it as physical activity (expenditure of energy). This something is the connection of work to the creation of a product in accordance with a plan (idea).

Work of this kind has significance for the task of being a self. The product of work also has this significance when its use unifies self and object. When work has to do with utilizing the individual's talents and realizing the individual's projects, work realizes its own ideal. The unity of subject and object through work is not, however, inevitable. A split between the two develops when the end of work is disconnected from the subjective life of the worker. Then, the product becomes indifferent to the workers who participated in its production. We can speak in such cases of the alienation of labor, meaning this separation of object from subject.

Of course, in a market economy, the producer sells the product, and in this sense alienates it (separates it from self). Doing so does not entail, however, a split in the foregoing sense. So long as the product embodies the subjectivity of the producer, it unites subject and object even though the object becomes the property of another. Indeed acquisition by another can enhance the objectivity of the product by making its reality intersubjective. By making the product that much more objective, it makes the unity of subject and object that much more real.

Outside of work, the self can find an objective existence in the use of things. The set of things appropriate to express the self's inner nature can form a place in which individuals can be themselves. Economists refer to the things that help establish the space of the self in the world as means of consumption, which include the durable goods (especially the home) that shape and protect that space. To arrive at a meaningful notion of a just economy means to know the basic principle governing work and place in the world.

Where work and place are meant to fit the individual, markets take on special significance. Markets for labor offers individuals freedom to participate in determining the kind of work they do in accordance with their abilities and interests. Markets for goods provide individuals with the opportunity to find and acquire those things suitable to express and realize their senses of self. The system of private property right secures the attachment of labor and goods to persons as their private property.

But, the primacy of the market, particularly the labor market, also poses problems. The labor market makes welfare contingent on the sale of laboring capacities. The exchange of labor for money can fail for various reasons, including the worker's failure to develop capacities valued in the market, and the market's failure to offer employment even to those with capacities of value. Both of these failures have relevance for justice since both undermine the individual's sense of self and with it his or her capacity to maintain relations with others based on mutual regard. If we bear in mind the link between regard for others and regard for self, we can see more in market failure than a threat to individual welfare. This relevance of market failure to the concerns of justice supports two limitations on the market. The first has to do with unemployment, the second with welfare.

Labor markets can provide a degree of individual choice, and thus self-determination. They do so when individual's have capacities valued by those offering employment, when there exists a sufficient number of employers to prevent coercion, and when product markets work well enough to generate adequate demand for labor. When these conditions do not hold, labor markets can undermine rather than assuring self-determination. Thus the relation between labor markets and justice is a complex one. Much of this complexity has to do with the threat of unemployment faced by those able and willing to work. Many contemporary labor markets are constructed on the assumption that without this threat workers will have little incentive to provide labor in quantity and quality adequate to do the work society needs done. The threat unemployment provides, then, is vital to efficient production.

Of course, the threat of unemployment only exists where unemployment exists. Since unemployment deprives the unemployed of their livelihood, efficiency based on a threat of deprivation seems to conflict with justice.[3] A simple, and in its way compelling response to this conflict would be to insist on the priority of justice over efficiency. To undermine justice is to erode the fabric of our life together, while to be inefficient only means that we have less to use and consume than we might otherwise have. Enough inefficiency will, however, undermine justice if justice depends, as I suggest below, on the overall capacity of the economy to provide adequate wealth. Undermining efficiency can threaten justice. Thus efficiency is a concern of justice, and the problem of the seeming tradeoff between the two cannot be so easily dismissed.

Another response insists that the threat of unemployment is unnecessary to assure the employee's devotion to work. Significant counter examples exist to the claim that work must be motivated by a convincing threat. Indeed, some theorists have argued that coercive forms of labor organization undermine efficiency (see Shapiro 1994). If this is correct, then coercing labor by threatening loss of income does not enhance wealth or otherwise support any conditions of justice linked to provision of adequate income.

These are powerful counterarguments that at least weaken the presumed conflict between justice and efficiency. They do so by finding an intrinsic motivation to put in place of the extrinsic motivation of the reward for work and the threat of its withdrawal. To find intrinsic motivation is to see value in the work itself. Whether we can find such intrinsic motivation depends on the kind of work. Clearly, work that, to some extent at least, embodies an element of the worker's selfhood has an intrinsic value to the worker independent of the extrinsic value of the pay received. However, work and its product do not always involve this moment of embodiment of self.

Those who favor the line of argument centering on the intrinsic value of work insist that there is meaning in a kind of work that has long been denounced as mind-deadening and self-denying.[4] I refer here to unskilled labor, for millennia associated with agriculture and in more recent history typical of industry, that provides little or no opportunity for self-expression and self-development. Because it entails separation of labor as activity from the laborer as a person, labor of this kind involves suppression of the self.[5] To labor in this way, the worker must put his or her subjective being aside: desires, interests, hopes, creative potential, and so on. This putting aside what makes the worker a person is done through an act of repression, usually referred to as self-discipline. Self-discipline, in this case, means repression because it runs contrary to the individual's interest in being him or her self. The more ubiquitous the separation of labor from the person of the laborer, the smaller the terrain of justice within the economy, the less the economy works as a support for a larger system of justice.

Widespread use of unskilled labor also challenges the justness of the economy because its remuneration tends to fall below a minimum demanded by the needs of the self. Because their work, and to that extent a substantial part of their lives, does not enable them to express or exercise their subjective being, to be themselves, workers engaged in unskilled labor tend to be treated as having lesser selves, therefore being of less worth. This justifies, even necessitates, their being paid less than others, even less than what is needed to be a person. If such labor is needed for the production of wealth, wealth production limits justice. Thus, while justice requires wealth, it also stands in conflict with it. Marx proposes the classic solution to this conflict. He imagines a situation where technological change increases labor productivity to the point where labor becomes unnecessary to the production of wealth. If unskilled labor is not needed to produce wealth, then production of the wealth required to secure justice need not conflict with justice.

Marx finds an obstacle to this solution in social arrangements assuring that no amount of wealth can be adequate. Under capitalism, accumulation of wealth becomes an end in itself. The limitless expansion of wealth means expansion in the need for labor to produce wealth even if the productivity of that labor increases.[6] Capital accumulation means enlisting labor in the production of wealth not because production of wealth is labor intensive, but because the amount of wealth needed grows without limit. No reduction in unit labor requirements can eliminate the need for labor if the demand for wealth expands rapidly enough to overwhelm the effect of any possible increase in labor productivity on the demand for labor.

Further, so long as income depends on the sale of laboring capacities, and so long as social arrangements do not assure that all (or virtually all) workers have skills enabling them to do the kind of work that secures self-esteem, the need for subsistence will drive many to offer their labor for low paid unskilled employment. Social arrangements, then, assure a supply of labor to jobs that cannot contribute to the self-feeling we associate with justice. Marx's critique is, appropriately enough, directed at those social arrangements that prevent elimination of the kind of work that produces a conflict between wealth and justice.

Marx's argument may be more relevant today than it was at his time. As the demand for unskilled labor in the production of goods diminishes, the supply of such labor flows into the service sector, and the economy divides into sectors of high skill high pay work and low skill low pay work. This movement is, to a degree, an artifact of differences in income and wealth rather than the exigencies of production. The (low wage part of the) service sector provides those with higher incomes an additional measure of freedom at the expense of those without skills who, because of the link between income and employment, must sell their labor for what they can get for doing what they must.[7]

Enough wealth

A conflict between wealth and justice arises when an adequate amount of wealth for the ends of justice cannot be produced without depriving some who produce it of at least part of what, as a matter of justice, is due them. At the heart of the conflict, then, is a judgment about how much wealth is enough to secure justice. Economics does not answer the question how much wealth is enough, but the classical economists do consider a related question: How much wealth can there be? Their answer centers on the idea that the accumulation of capital eventually reaches a limit, so that there can only be so much wealth.

David Ricardo saw the limit to wealth in the amount of fertile land available. Once all fertile land comes under cultivation, the cost of the worker's subsistence will equal the worker's product, and nothing will remain for investment in the means to produce more wealth.[8] Ricardo does not consider whether this amount of wealth is enough in our sense. As it turns out, the workers are not better off producing more than they were when they produced less, although during the process of accumulation they find their situation temporarily improved so far as their wage is concerned. Once accumulation ends, their prospects dim considerably.

Other than rejecting the idea that fertility limits growth, Marx does not take us much further than Ricardo. In place of natural limits, Marx argues that wealth accumulation is limited by the mechanization of production, which tends to reduce the rate of profit, blunting the stimulus to gain (as he puts it), and thus extinguishing the motive for investment in the means to produce more wealth.

It is not, however, only the stimulus to gain that is blunted in this way. On the contrary, if Marx is right and the ratio of net product to capital invested falls as capital grows, the rate of growth of wealth will decline whether means of production are privately owned and decisions made on the basis of profitability or not. Here, too, we must eventually reach the point where we have all the wealth we can. But, having reached this point because of the characteristics of technology, there is no reason to suppose that all the wealth we can have will be enough. Like Ricardo, Marx offers little to guide us in knowing how much wealth is enough.

The lacunae in the classical theory concerning how much wealth is enough stems from a weakness in that theory's treatment of the normative basis of economic organization. Because ethics plays at best an implicit role, the question how much wealth is enough cannot be answered, or for that matter explicitly posed. The place, however, where normative considerations clearly enter is in the specification of the workers' subsistence.

If we take the classical notion of subsistence seriously, the classical economists must believe that enough wealth is the amount that provides workers with their subsistence, which (according to the classical thinkers) depends on historical and cultural (or 'moral') factors we can only describe given a particular time and place. Introduction of these factors was meant to suggest that workers have a way of life embedded in a cultural reality whose demands carry moral force. That is, to pay the worker less than he needs to preserve the way of life appropriate to his being a worker in a particular cultural milieu would be immoral (see Stirati 1994).

As the classical economists understand, this implies that consumption habits built up over time create not just expectations, but obligations. Enough wealth would, then, mean approximately the amount that the workers have lately been in the habit of consuming, which might be very little, or it might be moderately substantial depending on circumstances. However, if this is true, then justice cannot stand opposed to wealth, at least in principle. By this definition of subsistence, it must be possible to produce enough wealth, since enough is as much wealth as we have been in the habit of providing.

If we hold to some version of the classical idea of subsistence, then any conflict between justice and efficiency (or productivity) is not inherent, but an artifact of the conditions that make the subsistence for some reason either inadequate or unavailable. These are the conditions connected with unemployment, or with the emergence of a need for wealth, luxuries, and riches. So far as part of society has this need, the fact that the economy can provide subsistence does not mean it can provide enough wealth to satisfy wants and assure justice.

The classical economists tended to identify the need for wealth (beyond subsistence) with a class division in society.[9] While subsistence might be adequate to members of the working class, it is not adequate to those who face the prospect of acquiring more. Still, both Smith and Ricardo judge wants to be unlimited for all persons, including members of the working class. Ricardo uses this idea to counter Say's Law (Ricardo 1951, pp. 293-4).

Smith and Ricardo argue that while the desire for any particular object may be limited, since in acquiring it the need it meets can be satisfied, this does not mean that the desire for objects in general will ever be satisfied, since that desire can settle on an ever changing and expanding set of objects. In effect, classical economics divides want into two kinds. The first is for specific, finite objects linked to particular need and use. The second is want in general, which, since it does not fix on particular things, has no limit.

This idea of want in general tends to undermine the classical solution to our problem, which links ideas of subsistence and limits to growth in determining how much wealth is enough. The idea of want in general is connected to two aspects of want that tend to be corrosive of the classical method based on an idea of subsistence. The first is the diversity of consumption patterns across individuals; the second is the growth of wealth beyond the limits anticipated in the classical theories. The idea that the subsistence is enough loses coherence when consumption patterns vary widely from worker to worker both in composition and amount. And, the idea that enough is as much as there can be (or has been) helps very little when how much there can be increases seemingly without limit.

If the classical theory does not help us, how might we discover how much wealth is enough for the ends of justice? To answer this question, we must know more about the need wealth satisfies than the classical idea of subsistence tells us. The classical theory's failure begins with its failure to explore more fully the kinds of need appropriate to wealthy (or, for Smith, civilized) society. It is not that the classical economists are wrong when they insist (at least implicitly) that enough wealth is the amount that assures subsistence; it is that their way of thinking about subsistence tends to exclude its recipients from the way of life required for self-determination, and thus for justice to prevail.

The classical idea excludes recipients of subsistence from civilized life and full access to justice precisely because their subsistence does not provide for the multiplication and individuation of need, and therefore for the true needs of the self. In the next section, I explore the kinds of need implied in a civilized life, and their implications for understanding the limits of the market.

The limits of the market

Public and private

I suggest above that the security of private property is a matter of its limits. To understand the limits of property, we will need to understand better the distinction between public and private. Here, I will explore a limited part of that distinction, the part specifically bound up with private property and the nature of the attachment of goods to persons it implies.

What makes our relation to a good private? The excludability criterion employed in public goods theory has to do with the capacity of the consumer to appropriate or attach the good to him or her self. If we interpret appropriability as attaching to the person, the criterion of appropriability remains ambiguous until we define more closely the relevant attributes of the person. There are many such attributes. We can, for example, consider the different meaning and implication of the person's physical and psychic being, or familial and professional being.

With regard to the former distinction, consider medical care. The care an individual receives when ill can be attached to and appropriated by that individual, at least in an important sense. If the broken arm is mine, then so also is the care needed to repair it. Yet, such care may have little to do with my particular attributes as *this* person. It does not express or live out who I am. The good I need (medical treatment) may not be attachable to the particular or unique dimensions of my personality. Whether it is or not bears on its relation to my self-interest, and on the argument that it be treated as private property.

The question of attachability to person also arises in the context of education. How we judge, for example, the desirability of privatizing education depends on how we judge the aspect of personality to which we attach it. Here, it is not a matter of physical versus psychic. Instead, the distinction that carries weight is between the personality's universal and particular dimensions. That is, education can be an attainment common to all who aspire to be fully persons in a community of persons. Or, education can be an attainment linked to the particular talents and interests of individuals, and the life plans developed out of those talents and interests.

In the first (universal) dimension, education develops abilities and knowledge held in common within the community. The knowledge and abilities may be a means to bind members to the group via shared culture; or, they may be universal requirements of self-determination (for example, the ability to read and write) important to the degree the community values autonomy in its citizens. In the second (particular) dimension, education develops abilities that mark differences between persons. Professional or vocational education develops talents and interests so they may form the basis of a career. Since kind of work connects to the particular aspect of personality, choice plays an important role. Where choice plays a role, the market can be a significant institution.

Where education attaches to the universal dimension, the differences fostered by market provision and choice are not only irrelevant, but potentially harmful. Because of this, two conservative education policies must part company. One policy insists on greater educational choice, for example by expanding private at the expense of public education through the use of educational vouchers intended to shift public funds to the private sector. A second policy insists on the redirection of curriculum away from diversity and choice toward a common core students will all experience to assure they develop the knowledge and skills demanded by their community and culture. Core curriculum, because it diminishes the part played by choice, offers less space for arguments favoring use of markets. To resolve the matter of the role and limits of the market in the area of education, we must know how education connects to the student, or, in our language, to what dimension of personality the education attaches itself. Then, we can judge the use and limits of the market, and the desirability of treating education as part of the property system.

By the criterion of attachability to the self, neither medical care nor (universal) education may be goods of the same order as clothes or other personal objects. This does not, of course, make either a public good on the same plane as parks and highways.[10] Instead, they occupy a third category: goods bearing a relation to self-interest different from that relation implied in the simpler two-fold distinction favored in the public goods literature. The criterion of attachability to the person becomes multidimensional when the notion of the person is allowed to exhibit different aspects. This leads to a more complex approach to the problem of what is public, what private.

Property

At the center of the problem of social justice and the limits of the market is the matter of attachability of good to person. Underlying this issue is the concept of the person and of the facets of personality as they define the connection of person to object. In this section, I briefly explore approaches to this problem important in the early history of political economy.

A notion of attachment of object to person anchors the Lockean theory of property right. For Locke, right followed the investment of labor in forming the object, its transformation from the materials into something useful, which bears meaning and significance in human practice. To be sure, Locke tended to understand this meaning in a language that obscured its social determination. Still, his theory treats property right on the basis of attachability.

This attachability follows investment or embodiment. The person embodies his personality in the object through its production process. Such an idea makes more sense the more the object bears the mark of its producer, that is, the more we can discern the personality of the worker in the shape of the product. In handcraft production and in art, this is normally the case. While Locke does not restrict the application of his principle in this way, the language he uses to convince the reader that laboring constitutes a claim to its object is one that emphasizes the residue of the laborer in the object. The laborer's person is somehow in the thing. We might interpret this in a formal juridical sense. Recognition of the object as property makes it a container for the personality of its owner. But, this reverses the order of determination that motivates Locke's argument.

The handcraft assumption helps since it defines an embodiment not directly derivative of juridical personality and ownership. In handcraft production, the shape or design of the object contains the plan originally in the mind and skill of the producer. We can tell who produced it from the form of the product. Thus, we can identify the work of the particular Anasazi craftsman from the remains of the pottery produced hundreds of years ago. The product bears the imprint of its producer.

I will take this idea as a possible archetype of attachment as that is relevant to political economy. The idea proposed by Locke has close ties to the classical labor theory of value, except that for the latter the normative element is missing or suppressed. Smith attempts to argue for labor time as the determinant of exchange value not on the grounds that laboring constitutes a basis for right, but on the grounds that given the right of the laborer over his labor, he will only part with its product for another requiring a comparable expenditure of labor to produce. Smith takes the right of the laborer to his product for granted, and concerns himself with the rates at which properties exchange in relation to the labor used in their production.

The classical theory assumes what Locke attempts to demonstrate: the right of the producer to his product. Taking this right for granted becomes problematic, of course, when the laborer does not own his product, as is normally the case under a capitalistic system of production, where laboring capacity is sold in the market for a wage. Once the laboring capacity is sold to another (the capitalist), we need to know who is the rightful owner of the product.

By simplifying Locke's argument, we can arrive at the conclusion that the rightful owner of the product of labor must be the owner of the labor (which, subsequent to the wage contract, is the capitalist). The needed simplification involves separating labor from the personality of the worker. Then, embodying labor into the product does not imply any connection of the product to the personality of the laborer. If right still follows embodiment of labor, then right to the product goes to the owner of the labor, who is not the laborer.

This alteration in the original argument would seem to fit where the organization of production obliterates the imprint of the producer's personality on the product. Capitalist economic organization separates product from laborer. Legally, the product belongs to someone other than the laborer who worked on it. Substantially, the product does not embody qualities of that laborer's personality. Capitalist production is organized to assure that the worker's personality is not involved.[11] Marx refers to this condition as 'abstract' labor. Indeed, the notion of abstract labor is essential to the classical labor theory of value employed by Marx.

Still, Marx insists that the worker has a claim to the product. While recognizing that legally the product belongs to the owner of the capital, Marx wants to argue that the value claimed by that owner is the result of exploitation of labor. Exploitation refers to the appropriation of value produced by another, in this case by the worker.

Marx separates the idea of exploitation from that of right, so that the wrong associated with exploitation is not that it violates right. This is a difficult separation to maintain. It likely stems from a narrow notion of justice as a purely legal or judicial concept.[12] In light of this narrow concept of justice, the wrong implied in exploitation cannot be that it violates right, since legally it does not. Nonetheless, it still violates the integrity of the worker by subjecting him or her to domination by the owner of the capital.

Domination of this kind may be just in a positivist sense. That is, it may conform with existing laws, including laws deeply embedded in the logic of a particular economic order, which protect the contracts that enable capitalists to exploit workers. This does not mean, however, that domination is just if justice is something more than simply the legal expression for economic conditions. In any case, it is difficult to imagine a meaningful use of the term domination that does not appeal, however implicitly, to the ethical concerns embodied also in the idea of justice.[13] The ideal of justice may be well or poorly instantiated under existing conditions. Clearly, justice in the sense of respect for the integrity of the other is violated by the relation of servitude one student of Marx sees as the essence of exploitation (Wood 1972).

Problems for the classical theory of value and property arise when the product does not embody the personality of its producer. This happens in part because of the changing role of the means of production. The latter come to embody the plan and idea for the product, so that the laborer's contribution loses its formative role, becoming so much abstract labor time.

At this point, we can follow the juridical notion of attachment, arguing that property follows a recognized attachment to a formal, juridical personality. If we, then, treat the product of labor as that same labor in an altered form, it follows that whoever owns the labor has the right to the product. Ownership, considered as a relation between personality and thing, is, then, a formal matter. The only dimension of personality relevant to a claim of property right is the juridical dimension.

We cannot have a system of right, especially property right, if we do not recognize this dimension. It does not follow, however, that recognizing it provides us with all we need for a system of property right. Some have argued that it does (Nozick 1974). Doing so resolves the problem of the limits of the market in accord with a notion of justice. The rights that define the market system are only limited by those considerations bearing on the transfer of rightfully owned property.

The more abstract and formal the conception of personality deemed relevant to property right, the fewer restrictions that conception allows on its exercise, the less it has to say about what we can or cannot do with property, what sorts we can or cannot own, and what claims we might have over things we do not own. Even assuming, as we must, the necessity of this dimension to any meaningful theory of the market, we are not required to end our exploration here or avoid introduction of other dimensions of personality conceivably relevant to a justice centered approach to the question of the limits of the market.

The next step, however, raises considerable difficulty. It requires us to consider the person not simply as the locus of right, but also as a complex of wants or needs (Hegel 1952, pp.122-3). We also attempt to justify and make real our attachment of things to ourselves in the dimension of want. This is particularly important in the history of market economy. It involves the key issue of the nature of the claim wanting creates to its object. Can we claim a right to something because we want it? Because we need it?

The question, if we are to answer it in the affirmative, immediately concretizes the entire matter of property right and its relation to personality. This makes it inherently problematic in a market system that depends heavily on abstraction of personality. Indeed, this abstraction is one of the market's great accomplishments.

Some critics of the market attack it for the way it abstracts from the concreteness of persons. Their charge is, of course, not entirely accurate. The idea of the market is that it will make possible the expression of personality in its concreteness without infringing on the process by which person's define their wants and goals. To do so, the market need not know the person, or be concerned with why that person wants what he or she wants. The market does not know how compelling need is, or where it originates. It does not measure needs except by the amount of money we are willing to part with to satisfy them, which can depend as much on the amount of money we have as on how important the object is to us. It remains the case that the market is designed not to know who we are. In this sense, it treats us abstractly.

Rejecting the abstraction of personality takes us away from grounding our argument about the market in the notion of justice because it disconnects want satisfaction from self-determination. Treating personality immediately in all its concreteness makes us lose track of the individual's freedom to make want satisfaction a matter of his or her acting and willing. Any coherent justice centered approach to the limits of the market entails treating persons in abstraction from particularity in order to make the process of particularization their own. Without this kind of abstraction, the market would not face limits, it would disappear. Let me return, then, to the project of linking property right to want or need within a conception including a notion of abstract personality.

We cannot do this without thinking more concretely about the kinds of wants relevant to the market, and thinking this way directly presumes that some wanting is relevant, some not. To fix ideas, I will begin with the idea of need in classical political economy.

Subsistence

As we have seen, the dominant reference point for need in classical political economy is 'subsistence'. This notion is subject to various interpretations. What, I think, stands out, is that subsistence is given independently of the self-definition of wants.[14] Some classical and classically inspired theories interpret the subsistence in physical/natural terms, placing it, in Piero

Sraffa's words, on a par with 'the feed for the cattle' (1960, p. 9). We know it from needs human beings have as part of their species, needs for nutrition, clothing, shelter. More often, classical theories attempt to include things wanted for other reasons, introducing elements variously termed cultural, historical, or social. Whether natural or cultural, the subsistence consists of a bundle of goods required to sustain or reproduce the worker, perhaps within an historically given setting. The worker's experience of the market has nothing, in principle, to do with the composition and size of the subsistence basket. The market is one mechanism among many for providing workers with the things they need.

When the worker's need is met by subsistence, what he needs follows not from who he is, but from the class to which he belongs. This fits either within a physiological or cultural conception. Physiologically, what we need has little to do with who we are in ourselves (except perhaps for how big we happen to be). Culturally, if the subsistence follows general cultural patterns given to the member, the need satisfied by it has little to do with who the member is in him (or her) self.

The need we satisfy through the subsistence is given to us, not determined by us. It is made for us but it is not of us; it is not our own. Put another way, the determination of want comes to us from outside; it is not a part of our self-determination. Small wonder, then, that the market is inessential to the concept of the subsistence and the concept of need connected to it.

The subsistence, then, attaches not to our inner core of selfhood, but to attributes we share with others of our species or class. These may, in some sense, be meaningful dimensions of personality to which we need to attach objects. They dictate the use of relevant objects needed to establish our sameness with others, and to keep our bodies whole. If, however, they are the whole of our wants, no very strong argument can tie their satisfaction to the market. The market has nothing to do with the wants themselves; it is, rather, a technique for satisfying them. Nothing in the concept of subsistence requires that we own its elements as our private property. This follows from the nature of its attachment to us, and from the dimension of our persons to which it is attached. Because of this quality of subsistence, it constitutes a poor candidate for the work of the market and the property system. If we cannot establish any necessity for us to own the elements of the subsistence as our private property, we cannot establish any necessity for the market as provider of the things we need.

Marx recognizes this quality of want when he treats the market as a mechanism for appropriating surplus, rather than as something logically tied to provision of things to satisfy a certain class of wants. In his economic writings, Marx treats the worker as a kind of wage slave. He has the wants of a slave, but acquires the things to satisfy them differently. He receives money from his employer, and uses it to buy back the subsistence goods he has himself produced. The exchange encourages the illusion that the laborer is a free man, master of his destiny, property owner on the same level as the owner of capital. But this is an illusion. In actuality, the worker gets nothing more or better than the slave.

To be sure, Marx understands more than this. Still, he constructs his economic arguments, following the classical economists, as though he has forgotten the more he once understood. He ends up seeing the market as a mechanism, want as emanating out of class identity and physiology. Because of this, considerations having to do with rights play a small part in his thinking about the limits of the market.

The idea of subsistence has relevance to the debate over planned economy. Clearly certain ideas about the planning process entail a notion of subsistence interpreted in the sense outlined above. Their advocates seek to remove the satisfaction of wants from the vicissitudes of the market, so far as possible. Removing want satisfaction from the vicissitudes of the market also removes want satisfaction from self-determination. Organizing the planned economy to minimize the role of the market has foundered on the implications of doing so for the self-determination of want.

Self-determination of want

To understand the place of the market in want satisfaction, we need to identify relevant dimensions of personality. In this, the classical notions fail us. The reason they fail is, however, illuminating. The subsistence idea, whether physiological or cultural, locates the determination of want outside the person, in nature and in culture. The market becomes meaningful when the determination of want originates within.

This claim takes us onto a troubled terrain. Inside and outside suggests a topological depiction of personality. The significance of the language has to do with a distinction between what comes from within, and what comes from outside. So, the problem of the market engages us in the problem of understanding what it means for want to come from within, and what within us is the source of wants that are our own.

This something within is the moving force or spirit of personality, referred to above as the self. The determination of want from within is also the self-determination of want, by which we mean the determination of want by the self. The question about want, whether physical, psychic, or social (and human want by its nature combines the three), is its relation to the self. The question about the market is about its relation to the wants of the self. To understand the limits of the market, we must understand the different ways different wants connect to, or emanate out of, the self.

The answer given us in contemporary social science is that all want connects to the self in the same way, that different wants are variations on a single theme of wanting. All we want is satisfaction, and satisfaction is the same thing and carries the same meaning no matter what happens to be its specific object (something to eat, medical care, social status). All want provides, and all want can provide, is a measure of satisfaction.[15]

Thinking in this way obscures the qualitative dimension of want. Satisfaction of want has a meaning that varies with the kind of want, which varies with the aspect of the self to which the want connects. Leaving aside the qualitative aspect, and the connection of want to an internally differentiated self, impedes the effort to interpret the limits of the market on the basis of a notion of social justice.

To link up with a conception of social justice, we need to think about the connections of want to self differently. How the self participates in the satisfaction of its wants depends on the kind of want. Only a certain kind of want connects to the self in a way that makes the market relevant (Hegel 1952, pp. 127-8). It is not a matter of the measure, but of the kind of satisfaction, which depends on the dimension of the self involved in the want to be satisfied, on the different ways the self relates to its own wants.

Considering the relation of the self to its wants can take us in two different directions. The first treats wants as drives emerging independently of our social condition, that is without concern for the regard for others and for selfhood that establishes the basis for social being. The second treats what we want as essentially a social condition. This latter is what we mean by the self-determination of want; it refers us to a want that incorporates the connection to the self understood not only as a particular (our self) but also as a universal (selfhood as such).[16]

This universal recalls the importance of the universal aspect of personality in understanding the nature and determination of property. We cannot treat property exclusively in relation to the particular dimension of personality, simply as a connection to particular want, without weakening its link to the self and its determination as a unity of the particular and universal.

Needs, wants, and private property

Let me briefly consider some examples of the ways objects connect to persons to see how differences in mode of connecting parallel different kinds of want and different dimensions of personality. I will give special attention to the nature of the attachment of object to person that makes that object a likely candidate for provision through exchange.

Consider ownership of unimproved land. By fencing in a piece of land, I can exclude others from access to it (incidentally fulfilling a condition that defines what is private in the public goods theory). If my right to the land, and thus to fence it in, is recognized, the property is attached to me in a legal sense. Recognition makes my land my private property, although there is nothing substantively private about it. By substantively private, I have in mind the connection of the land to those of my qualities that by their nature exclude others. This is the terrain of the self others might find alien because it is not them. Others enter such terrain by invitation, and only when their own qualities dissipate the alienation many would experience there.

If this is an important part of what we mean by private, then private property means those things that help to make the terrain of the self exclusive in this sense. Unimproved land may be appropriable in a juridical sense, depending on the nature of existing law governing land ownership, but it is not the kind of good that attaches to the private dimension of the self. Its claim to be private property is therefore questionable.

For property to become substantively private it must become part of the terrain of the self. Christopher Bollas speaks of this terrain when he refers to 'the discrete living villages (composed of all those objects we select to cultivate our needs, wishes, and interests) that we create during our lifetime' (1989. p. 9). If the creation of a world for ourselves is our purpose in owning property, and this makes sense of the notion of *private* property, then this tells us something important about the kinds of things that are suitable for private ownership.

Such objects must be capable of taking on a meaning within our modes of life (see Levine 1988, chapter 1), in relation to who we are, and in relation to the other objects we use to establish a space for ourselves. If they are to express who we are, such objects must be chosen by us. The market is uniquely designed to enable us to make choices that create a world of the sort alluded to here. The market produces goods without knowing who will buy them, or how they will become part of that person's mode of life. Yet those products, once taken into the framework of that life, have a meaning that, in their use, connects the person to him or her self, and conveys the sense of that connection to others (Levine 1978, p. 190). Shirts, shoes, furniture, all have the capacity to contribute to the formation of the 'living village' referred to by Bollas. As such, they make sense as objects of exchange, provided to us at our initiative and according to our choices.

Now consider a different sort of example. When I break my leg, the crutches I use need not be mine. This is because my relation to them is not (or at least need not be) essentially private as I am using the term. The crutches are not constituents of my living village. When my leg is well, no sense of personal loss need attend my separation from them. Yet, crutches are not public goods. They are technically excludable in that their use connects them to the person using them and no one else. They do not serve a public interest. The need they satisfy is bound up with the interests of the self in its own (physical) well-being.

This last example suggests how connection to the self does not imply an argument for private appropriation, i.e. as private property. The self has different dimensions. That dimension identified with its private life bears a special connection to the idea of private property and therefore exchange. The other dimensions do not.[17]

We can use the language of need and want to capture the distinction discussed here; but, we must take care in doing so. Those trained in the economist's way of thinking make want accidental, need necessary. I have elsewhere questioned this way of drawing the distinction (Levine 1988, chapter 1). The distinction may, however, be meaningful if we are careful to bear in mind that the forces driving us to acquire the things we want, while different from those driving us to acquire what we need, are not therefore either less compelling or inherently capricious.

The distinction between need and want is a distinction in the way the absence of an object is felt by the self. The language helps distinguish in which of its dimensions the self feels diminished by that absence. Both need and want can be thought of as a call to action, or, to borrow from Freud, as a demand placed upon the mind for work. This call to action or demand for work (which is what we mean by the absence of an object) can be experienced in two ways: as an external imposition on the psyche, or as something the psyche imposes on itself. I will use the term need for the former, want for the latter. Thus, a need is imposed *upon*, a want is imposed *by*, the self. Both are in their way imperative, and, because of this, need remains the more general term, encompassing both instances. Yet, it will prove helpful to keep the terminological distinction along the lines suggested. While both are imperative, the imperatives differ.

When the call to action is imposed on but not by the self, choosing need not precede acting. But, when the call to action is imposed by the self, acting presupposes choosing. Put another way, choosing is the imposition of an action by the self on the self. Thus, the idea of a want as defined above entails choice.[18] The element of choice connects want to property and contract. The implied connection also makes the link between need and the market problematic. It is appropriate for a public authority to provide, by non market means, the things we need since, for them, the element of choice is not compelling. Self-interest, then, has at least two dimensions, one associated with want, one with need. The market bears a decidedly different connection to these distinct dimensions of interest.

Individual and social wealth

With the foregoing considerations in mind, let me return to the question raised earlier: How much wealth is enough?[19] Enough wealth would be an amount adequate to satisfy wants and needs. Wealth, then, must be divided into two parts, one directed to satisfying wants, the other to needs. I will refer to the first as individual and the second as social wealth.

The end of individual wealth is individuation, and thus the satisfaction of wants particular to the individual. The kind and amount of wealth needed for this varies across persons with variation in their wants. Here, the rule of difference, and even inequality in amount of wealth, holds.

This inequality would not create problems if it were reasonable to assume that individuals know what they want, which is to say know themselves, so that their wants would stem not from their perceptions of the wants of others or the implications of amount of wealth for esteem in the eyes of others, but from what it means to be a self. If this were the case, inequality of wealth would not imply inequality of personhood, or any ranking of persons in a hierarchy. It would simply express differences in personality, and the accidental implications those differences have for the amount of wealth persons need, given the differing costs of goods.

Concern with esteem in the eyes of others can, however, make the object of want a position in a ranking of persons. When it does, it brings with it a measure of personhood in wealth, and this tends to make the need for wealth unlimited. When we undermine the idea that the need for wealth is finite, we undermine the possibility that there can ever be enough wealth. Does this mean that we must exclude esteem as a consideration in the real needs of the self? Doing so is problematic, particularly in light of the emphasis we have placed on recognition of self and other.[20]

Gaining esteem in the eyes of self and other makes the self real and secure. Pursuit of esteem in the eyes of others cannot, then, be inherently a problem for justice. But, when esteem is made contingent on relative amount of wealth, so that wealth measures worth, the relation between seeking esteem and justice becomes problematic. If esteem is pursued on this basis, its recognition (in self) is also its denial (in others). When recognition of those with more means denial for those with less, the pursuit of self-esteem can conflict with the pursuit of justice.

The unity of recognition and denial undermines self-determination at both poles. This is because the self's need for recognition becomes a need for recognition not of its talents and accomplishments as such, but of their rank in relation to those of others. In this recognition, the self risks a greater loss: that of a reality of its own, an identity recognized by others but not reduced to a mere matter of relative magnitude measured along a common dimension. Here also, wealth is a great leveller, obliterating as it does the real differences between persons, and making even those who have wealth subordinate to it.

When esteem is subject to measurement by amount of wealth, it has no upper limit. Because it gets tied to wealth, the want stemming from the desire for esteem also has no limit. By contrast, an esteem that might be attained without its loss on the part of others is a qualitative rather than quantitative matter. If self-esteem is defined in this way, it would be reasonable and feasible to provide wealth according to want, feasible because wants would be self-limited, and a finite amount of wealth would provide people with as much as they want.[21] Needless to say, this tends not to be the case. If it is not, then, providing individuals with as much wealth as they want requires an unlimited supply. The problem stems, as Thorstein Veblen emphasizes, from the use of wealth to measure personhood. So long as wealth measures worth, mutual recognition of self and other, and thus justice, demands equality of (individual) wealth, even though such equality also violates justice by denying the differences between persons a system of justice is meant to secure.[22]

This is an important tension, but not in the concept of justice. It is, rather, a tension between the ideal of justice (which includes satisfying individual wants so far as they are part of self-determination) and the reality of social organizations premised on (and contributing to) the absence of adequate means for the production of wealth to satisfy wants. Adapting the concept of justice to conditions of scarcity, as implied in justice as fairness for example, brings the ideal down to the ground, so to speak. It defines justice not as what should given what can be, but as what should be given what is. It defines justice given social arrangements that do not create enough wealth, that discourage discovery of the real (finite) wants of the self, and that subordinate some to the production of wealth for others.

While the end of individual wealth is want satisfaction, the end of social wealth is the satisfaction of need. The amount needed is the amount that will be adequate *equally* to satisfy needs since, if needs are unequally satisfied, inappropriate differences between persons are endorsed, and justice cannot be served. Yet, different persons have different needs, and here too justice does not imply equality of wealth. Some need more health care; some need more or more expensive education; and some, of course, live longer. Where needs are concerned, equality means that so far as needs can be and will be satisfied, they are satisfied for all.[23] This means equality even in the face of the implied differences demanded by justice.[24]

The argument for equality of need satisfaction (in the sense just outlined) has a root in the concern for security of the self introduced earlier. There, I suggest that the problem for a social policy rooted in justice is to create an environment of safety, where wants and needs can be satisfied, and where their satisfaction, if appropriate, is a matter of individual willing and acting. Of course, the special relation of need to self attenuates the role of choice. Because of this, individuals can be made secure if satisfaction of need is less a matter of their will than would be the case for want. Thus, social provision of the things needed out of social wealth is consistent with justice.

The distinction between need and want can also assist us in thinking about the nature and limits of the welfare system by providing a justification for non market provisioning of need that does not infringe on individual self-determination. A more thorough investigation of the nature and implication of need can help to define the role of a welfare system that does not violate the integrity of persons because it respects the distinction between want and need.

The ideas just outlined allow us to narrow the concept of private interest. Political economy tends to equate private ends with self-interest, and thus with the whole set of individual ends, with whatever the individual feels he needs or wants. But, private end makes more sense given a narrower interpretation, as one part of individual want, that part emanating out of the particularity of the self. This narrowing of the concept of private interest vis a vis self-interest is the first step toward identifying the limits of the market within a framework of social justice.

Wealth and justice

If we have enough wealth, or, more precisely, are able to produce enough wealth without violating the integrity of the worker in the process of production, then an important condition for justice is satisfied. If we cannot, or do not, produce enough wealth, or if we produce it in a way that denies the integrity of its producers, then we lack a necessary condition for a just society.

The same point can be made in the language of scarcity. Scarcity of wealth means unsatisfied want. If the want unsatisfied is connected to the integrity of the self, that is if it is not a mere preference but a real want, then scarcity means deprivation.[25] Deprivation means that the self is not secure in its world in the most basic sense. Thus, the concern justice has with security makes justice depend on wealth.

The problem is, of course, that social arrangements can assure that no amount of wealth can ever be enough. This happens when wealth measures worth and wealth accumulation is perceived as the route to the only kind of security possible: the security that comes with having more wealth, and thus more esteem. Having more brings the hope of security because self worth has been made relative and measurable. Then, having less than others threatens, and ultimately diminishes, our self-worth, making us insecure in the most essential sense: insecure in our selves.

The problem of distributive justice arises in a world of scarcity. The questions that arise in such a world are: Who will be deprived? What limits the allowable extent of relative deprivation? By what procedures will deprivation be allocated among persons? The idea that differences in wealth that imply deprivation can be just is the core idea of theories of distributive justice. Yet, this idea may not be correct. That is, if justice requires security, and security requires that wants and needs can be (though not necessarily that they will be) satisfied, scarcity impedes justice. Asking about distributive justice, then, is asking for justice where a basic condition of justice is not met.

The term justice is often applied where some of its conditions are not met. We might, for example, ask what is the just treatment of slaves, meaning by that the treatment consistent with their status as slaves. Justice as dueness sometimes works this way. If we accept this notion of justice, then, just differences in wealth conform to the differences in status between persons (or between persons and slaves). Yet, while the slave who receives his due in this sense is not deprived of what he needs to be a slave, he clearly is deprived of what he needs to be a person.

Indeed, this is exactly the point. We can make deprivation just if we accept that some are persons and some are not. If, however, we consider justice the way of life with others (that is, other persons) then we cannot reconcile justice with deprivation. We can only avoid this result, by diminishing or eliminating the link between scarcity and deprivation. We do so when we reconcile justice with scarcity by transforming need and want into preference, thereby assuring that integrity (of the self) is not at stake in our effort to satisfying want.

Many embrace the conclusion that little is at stake for the individual in want satisfaction. On one side, those who interpret want in the language of preference clearly seek to separate want from the integrity of the agent who wants. On the other side, those who reject notions of freedom tied to choice interpret the wanting tied to exchange as an example of false need. Market systems foster false needs that are not really needs of the self, but needs imposed on the self by others, particularly by those who hope to make a profit by fostering needs for the goods they produce. The ideas of preference and false needs have in common the separation of want from the integrity of the self who wants. Both insist that failure to satisfy want will not leave the individual diminished in any significant way. Indeed, for those who embrace the idea of false needs, the failure to satisfy those needs, far from leaving the consumer diminished, is the first step toward his or her liberation.

If the ideas about want, need, and their connection to the self just outlined carry force, we will need to reconsider the usual way of framing the question of economic justice in the language of distribution, with its connotations of scarcity and deprivation. Doing so need not avoid noticing the reality of a world where means are in some sense scarce, and many are deprived. What it might do, however, is question the project of finding a path to justice within that reality. The program of distributive justice (including justice as dueness, fairness, and equality) has been to find such a path. If we reject this program, our project might be the different, though not wholly unrelated, one of understanding the relation between justice as a normative ideal, and the process of economic development which, though it might lead toward the ideal, and even incorporate it as an end, is not just in itself.

The process of capital accumulation, and therefore the institutions of a capitalist economy, have been centrally implicated in the project of economic development toward a situation where justice in the stronger sense might be possible. In political economy, the key division has not been between the parts of wealth destined to satisfy wants and needs, but between the part destined for consumption and the part destined to enhance the capital stock, and thus future levels of production. Enhancing the capital stock by devoting a part of the product to new capital goods makes sense if the capital stock we have cannot produce enough wealth. This can be for either of two reasons. It can be because no amount of wealth can ever be enough. Or, it can be because even finite wants and needs linked to the security and autonomy of the self cannot be satisfied with the wealth we can produce given the capital stock we have. Knowing which of these two conditions holds is no easy matter, which means that knowing when the process of economic growth has achieved its end is also no easy matter.

Clearly, however, the knowledge we need is not empirical but normative. It stems from a conception of personhood, and of what being a person demands by way of access to wealth. One of the weaknesses of political economy has been its failure to articulate a meaningful and substantial conception of persons capable of providing the knowledge we need to answer the question how much wealth is enough.

Limits of growth

In an earlier part of this essay, I reviewed some classical solutions to the problem of the limits to growth. These solutions are less helpful than they might be because they do not take want (and thus demand) into account. Instead, they seek the limits to growth exclusively on what we might today refer to as the 'supply side'. These are limits set by the amount of fertile soil available (Ricardo), or by declining profitability due to increasing capital intensity (Marx), rather than limits involving wants. Thus, the classical approach tends to separate the problem of the limits to growth from the normative issue raised here concerning when we have enough wealth to satisfy want.

The theory that displaces the classical at the end of the Nineteenth Century, while it raises the problem of demand explicitly, still solves the problem of the limits to growth primarily on the supply side. It does so by positing scarcity of resources as a premise, and defining the economic problem as allocation of scarce goods among competing wants. Here, again, the specific normative issue concerning how much wealth would be enough cannot be posed clearly. We can begin to forge a link between the theory of economic growth and the normative issue raised here if we can make the system of want an important determinant of the accumulation process. Theories of what I have elsewhere termed 'market limited growth' (Levine 1978, chapter 4), because they incorporate want into the determination of the growth process, have relevance to the normative issue of when we have enough wealth, and how want can limit growth.

The central idea is that the accumulation of capital depends on both the quantitative and qualitative development of wants. In a system where wants do not change, as would be the case if they are for subsistence, growth could not be sustained. The change in want that fosters growth can be multiplication or expansion. That is, individual wants may change as part of the ongoing process of individuation, in which case change in want only means expansion so far as the population tends to increase; or, wants may change because, for each individual, more is better.

As I suggest above, more can be better either because we start out with too little wealth to secure individual integrity, or because wealth measures worth, and thus tends to increase as a means to enhance individual esteem. The end of growth comes, then, with the realization of two conditions.[26] First, the infrastructure of production has developed to the point where society has the capacity to produce enough wealth to secure personal integrity, without requiring that some engage in self-negating labor in the service of others. This is the ideal emphasized by Marx as capitalism's historical mission. Second, the end of growth comes with the realization on the part of the individual that the esteem he or she pursues in the eyes of others is neither relative nor quantitative. This requires a change not only in the self-ideal of the individual, but also in that of the community.

The change in the ideal of the self moves it away from one that differentiates particular selves quantitatively (by their wealth and income) to one that establishes a real particularization based on finite and unique self-ideals and life projects. This movement, then, brings the accumulation process to a close, since it is no longer fuelled by the transformation of ways of life ruled by the need for them to provide evidence of wealthiness. Understood in this way, the limit to growth is normative rather than technical or natural.

Private Enterprise

The issue just raised engages the debate over private ownership of the means of production, especially over the determinants of the amount and form of capital investment. The debate over private ownership of capital rarely, however, transpires on the terrain of justice. Discussion of the demise of planned economics in Eastern Europe and the Soviet Union supports this conclusion. While talk about liberty and efficiency dominates much of that discussion, this talk is well removed from the concerns of justice. The term liberty, when applied to the economy, recalls the liberty of commerce or free trade. Nothing intrinsic to this idea speaks to matters of self-determination (see Winfield 1988a, pp. 88-93), and therefore of social justice.

The debate over private enterprise touches on justice when it links incentives to payment or return in accord with contribution. The entrepreneur deserves his return not because the product bears his mark or attaches to his personality, but because he caused it to be made. He claims that socialization of the return means denial of the self (socialist rhetoric has, in its own way, been known to substantiate this claim).

I will not belabor the issue of payment in accord with productive contribution. I think it has very little analytical meaning either for the advocates or critics of private enterprise. In general, we cannot speak of or measure productive contribution independently of remuneration (for labor or capital), and therefore we cannot talk meaningfully about the equality or disparity between the two. The issue of incentives does, however, carry significance precisely because, at heart, it is an issue about validation of self-interest, and thus of the self. The classical arguments (usually associated with Adam Smith) tend to validate self-seeking as a means to ends other than the self, specifically growth of the national revenue.[27] If we accept the classical argument, we remain well removed from concerns of justice since self-determination is not the end, but the means. Private enterprise is not about self-determination, but about the use of self-interest (assumed innate) for public ends.

If, however, we consider the pursuit of self-interest intrinsically valid, the argument we associate with incentives takes on a new meaning, one closer to the concerns of justice. The demand that the self be rewarded for its efforts is a demand for its recognition and affirmation. This demand operates and grounds itself independently of concern that incentives guide individuals to socially desired ends. We need, then, to distinguish two aspects of income differences that may appear to be the same: incentives to work, and recognition of the self.

If wealth were abundant and wants finite, no question would arise concerning the measurement of productive contribution in relation to income, since each person could acquire as much income as he or she needed. Under these conditions, there would be no reason to shift income from one group to another. Yet, so long as work needs to be done to produce wealth, and so long as work (for some at least) entails self-denial, the problem of a relation between income and contribution cannot be wholly avoided. This is not the quantitative problem of measuring one in relation to the other, but the qualitative problem of not allowing some to avoid work while satisfying their needs using the product of the work of others.

Exploitation of those who work by those who do not can operate at opposite ends of the income spectrum. Some focus attention on those who do not or cannot work for a living, and must acquire what income they can as a transfer from those who can and do work. Thus, a critique of welfare rests on the insistence that income remunerate work. Others focus attention at the opposite end of the income spectrum. They point out that some need not work to acquire income because they gain income from their capital. Since they do not work, so far as income is the result of work, their income must come from the work of others.

Exploitation of those who work by those who do not poses a problem. Private enterprise is organized to eliminate one kind of exploitation and favor the other. For those who must work to live, private enterprise insists that income be tied to contribution.

The question of enough wealth defines a divide in thinking about justice in relation to income and wealth. If we do not have enough wealth, and if wants are not finite, the conditions for justice are not fully met. Speaking, then, of justice in income differences cannot avoid conundrums. By assuring justice along one dimension (for example want satisfaction) we assure injustice along another (for example separating remuneration from contribution). Conundrums such as this are inevitable when we attempt to use the criterion of justice where some of the conditions for justice are not satisfied.

The system we know as capitalism or private enterprise exists along the divide referred to in the last paragraph. Private enterprise raises the prerogatives of the self, and especially the dominion of the self over its products, to a governing principle; it insists that income be related to private property, that subsistence is not enough, that wants are not finite, that wealth is never abundant. Private enterprise, then, produces the many conundrums of income difference with which we are all too familiar. Does the connection between justice and recognition of the self and its prerogatives make private enterprise necessary to self-determination?

Marx's concept of capital proves helpful here (1967, chapter 4). Marx is careful not to identify capital with (produced) means of production, as is the habit in contemporary economics. Instead, he defines it as self-expanding value. Ownership of capital is, then, not about producing things, but pursuing wealth. In this framework, the question about private enterprise is best understood as a question about the pursuit of private accumulations of wealth. What part does such pursuit play in the work of self-determination? Does the incentive it offers involve an appeal to the self?

Much depends on our conception of the self, particularly on the nature of its social determination. The constitution of self in the recognition of others makes self-interest an achievement rather than an innate capacity. The extent of this achievement varies with the social world we inhabit, and with its capacity to recognize the self acting agent.[28] This recognition has, traditionally, had much to do with the way society conceives the boundaries that separate persons, and that mark out a private life in a world with others. These boundaries define what is inside and outside, to recall the topological metaphor introduced earlier.

Inside and outside become important as loci of action or agency. More specifically, they help us identify whether the ends pursued by the member should be thought of as self-determined or not. The answer depends on the existence of the self as a separable source or center of initiative (see Levine 1998). When the self has separated out in this sense, we can use the term not simply in the reflexive sense, but also as a noun referring to an entity in the world (albeit a subjective entity).

Within this framework, the question about capital becomes: Does the pursuit of private accumulations of wealth serve the ends of the self? It would help to know, when speaking of the role of the market in self-determination, what sort of self we have in mind. This is relevant because the notion of self-determination (taken substantively rather than formally) can only be applied once we know the nature of the self. This means we need to develop a more concrete conception of the self, and thus of the person, than that normally employed in thinking about the relation of private enterprise to self-determination.

The lack of concreteness in thinking about self-determination is most damaging to our effort to identify the limits of the market when it means we cannot know what we mean by the self, when it exists and when it does not, when it is real and when it only appears so. Bringing together what we know about the self as a mental structure with what we know about the idea of self-determination in the world of civil life would take us some steps toward a better understanding of the implications of social justice for the limits of the market.

Democracy and the market

Democracy as measure of the market

In thinking about economic institutions, it may prove tempting to make participation a criterion for judging the market and its limits. We do so when, as a matter of principle, we favor outcomes of the process of group deliberation based on equal political rights. When we judge institutions by the extent to which they instantiate the principle of group self-determination, we make democracy the measure of the market. But, what does democracy mean in connection to the economy? This question can be answered in more than one way. Here, I will distinguish two different answers.

The term democratic used with reference to economy might suggest something about how wants are formed, how they get satisfied, or how they impinge on political institutions and processes. If wants originate in the self, they can reinforce the autonomy presumed by democratic process. Satisfaction of self-determined wants involves a significant measure of choice, which is the type of action characteristic of a self-determined agent. Such links between democracy and economy do not make economic processes democratic. Democratic economy, on this interpretation, is not a democratically ordered economy, but one whose ordering principle is consistent with, and necessary to, democracy.

Alternatively, democratic economy might suggest that economic decisions be made democratically, using the appropriate kind and degree of participation and group self-determination. If democracy refers to a form of collective self-governance, thus to political process and institution, an economy can only *be* democratic if it is political.

Thus the issue of politicization of the economy enters the discussion of democracy and the market. Marx and the classical economists, of course, treat the economy as a depoliticized sphere. The idea of the economy as a non-political system, while central to the entire understanding of the original political economists, has recently been challenged by those who argue for a broader application of the notion of politics (see Offe 1987).[29] In order to sort through the issue of economy and democracy we must at the same time consider the limits of politics and the importance of a separate sphere of the economy protected from political action and process.

A non-political economy featuring the market might still be democratic if, as suggested above, it otherwise supports, or is somehow necessary to sustaining, democratic institutions outside the economy. Democratic economy in one sense refers to the organization of production and distribution, and to how they might be made to reflect full participation of appropriate groups. Democratic economy in the other sense refers to the design of economic institutions suitable to a democratic society.[30]

Those who call for democratization of economic institutions do so in part to assure greater equality, and to eradicate an important grounding for hierarchy. They also do so, however, in order to replace individual self-determination with group self-governance as a guiding principle of economic life. Thus, they suggest we extend the latter principle into what has been the primary domain of individuality. This assumes, of course, that the principle of democracy applies to the internal organization of an economy, which would be the case were we to make collective self-governance the fundamental value to be used in judging institutions.

The danger is that doing so depreciates the value of individual self-determination. In so-doing, the extension of democracy can undermine one of the most important roots of democracy in a free society, that is a society grounded in self-determination of persons. Eradicating unjust differences, and extending democracy into the economy, then, are not the same thing.

In thinking of participation, we should consider the expectations that come with self-determination. Does self-determination imply participation in management of enterprise, and if so in what way? Does it imply collective control of prices, quantities, methods of production, new product development, and so on? These are not the only important questions. Another has to do with identifying the appropriate group. Under capitalism, the appropriate group is the firm's Board of Directors, or possibly its shareholders. Advocates of economic democracy challenge the claims these groups make based on ownership in favor of a broader, but still microeconomic, determination of the appropriate governance group. Yet, as Walter Adamson (1990) points out, it is not obvious that firms should be specifically accountable to their employees.

The question of whose self-governance constitutes democratic self-governance carries weight. Which is the relevant group for decisions regarding the product mix of firms and for the economy as a whole? Which is the relevant group for decisions regarding the organization of production, the appropriate technology, the level of prices and wages, the rate of investment in plant and equipment, in research and development, in advertising, in product diversification? A decision regarding the amount of health care to produce can be decided by consumers, producers, private organizations (such as insurance companies), or by government. It may be no simple matter to determine which is the more democratic.

Decisions about how to produce may be made in worker managed firms by workers or their representatives. But it remains to be considered how the larger context of the market, and of public ends as embodied in government regulation and law, restricts those decisions. Increasing democracy within the firm may or may not make the economy more democratic, since the latter depends on whether those within the firm constitute the appropriate group for decision-making. At the same time, the significance of internal democracy depends on the extent to which important decisions can be relegated to the unit of production in a way consistent with public ends.

A related question has to do with the professions, and with the role of expertise. Members of professions also constitute groups relevant to the question of participation in decisions having economic significance. If democratization places decisions in the hands of all those affected, it limits the authority of the professions. We can, of course, ask when it is or is not wise to do so from the standpoint of consequences for economic ends: productivity, output, employment, and so on. We can also ask whether it is more or less democratic (see Sassower 1993). When those whose professional lives are devoted to relevant knowledge and judgment have that judgment overridden by a larger public, the sense of participation of the former group can erode. One arena of democracy is purchased at the cost of another. We need, then, to ask which is more salient. Does democracy enhance the prerogatives of the professions, or undercut them?

The answer to this question depends on our view of professional groups and associations. If we understand them to embody a kind of authority that negates the prerogatives of the citizenry, empowering them undermines democracy. But, if we understand professional groups to provide a vital link between individual self-determination and public ends, empowering them may actually support democratic institutions. Hegel and Durkheim argue that such groups raise their members to a higher ethical level by linking their private lives to an association cognizant of greater ethical ends. By doing so, private associations assure that civil society contains an explicit link to ethical order, and thus to public ends. On this understanding, empowering professional organizations binds public ends to individual self-determination. In turn, this helps assure that civil society is bound by the ends of ethical order, and that the public apparatus understands the prerogatives of civil society.

In the language introduced in the previous section, intermediate associations can help secure the link between the universal and particular aspects of self-interest. They do so by making more explicit the universal dimension of particular interest. In doing so, they combine the two moments. The resulting combination can make more conscious and explicit the universal underpinning of particular interest; but, it can also subject the universal to the corrupting influence of the particular.

Where the universal moment of self-interest is forced underground, and the particular strives to be the whole, as is often the case in economies organized around private ownership of capital, intermediate associations will be limited in their ability to link the two aspects of self-interest. Instead, they become instruments of particular interest. Then, intermediate associations may undermine democratic process by threatening the substance, if not the form, of democratic equality. The power of private associations, most obviously corporations and business or professional organizations, to skew outcomes in their *private* interest makes them a potential threat to democracy (see Brittan 1989 and Lindblom 1977).

This potential leaves us with a dilemma. On one side, intermediate associations support democracy by assuring that civil society contains a principle that transcends the pure pursuit of particular interest. On the other side, these same associations threaten democracy by intensifying inequalities originating in civil society, and making those inequalities the basis for political inequalities antithetical to democracy.

One of the long-standing claims for civil society is that it can absorb or defuse conflict. Civil society either (1) depoliticizes conflict by making it an essentially private matter, or (2) transmits conflict to the political arena in a form consistent with preservation of prevailing political and economic arrangements. In this sense, civil society constitutes a basis for social harmony. But it may not (see Hirst 1991).

Because of its commitment to the development of differences between persons, civil society can become the basis for social divisions that challenge the foundations of social organization. The point of the traditional account of civil society is that it encourages differences in order to avoid divisions. The differences between persons are so rooted, in their own capacities, decisions, and actions, that those differences reinforce the commitment to the larger social order that sustains them. However, if the differences that develop in civil society are not recognized to embody right in this sense, they can become divisions in society that threaten its overall cohesion.

Whether difference becomes the basis for division depends on whether some (or many) are excluded, and on the degree and kind of inequality differences imply. When civil society includes capitalist market economy, it tends to encourage the development of difference into division, at least up to a point. This is because capitalist market economy, by its nature, is only open to those who own something of value, where value is determined primarily, or even exclusively, by the market.

Nothing in the organization of the economy on this basis assures that anyone will have anything of value (including any labor of value) to sell, or that the price of what individuals own will be adequate to sustain them. At the same time, no limit exists to the wealth that can be amassed by those with property, talent, or good fortune. Indeed, since the primary means to the acquisition of wealth is wealth itself (especially capital), substantial inequalities, even poles of wealth and poverty, are more or less inevitable.

This indicates weaknesses in the structures of civil society and polity. These weaknesses have to do with the way the public authority enables the inequalities inherent in the private sphere to develop beyond a point consistent with the principle that the self-boundaries, which define personhood, be respected for all, a principle that underlies both a free civil society and a democratic polity. The weaknesses also have to do with the way the organization of the state makes it vulnerable to the influence of private interest.

Beyond these considerations, group self-determination within the economy runs up against an obvious and important limit: the role of the economy in providing the means for individual self-determination and self-expression. Thus, for example, the demand for worker self-management expresses the value of democratization of economic institutions. But, worker self-management encounters limits in that the firm, whether managed by workers or by corporate owners, remains a part of a larger economic organism dedicated to provision of things capable of satisfying wants and needs many of which remain individual in nature, and are the wants and needs of consumers not otherwise connected to the firm.

This does not make the idea of worker self-management irrelevant, but it does limit its applications to those consonant with the firm fulfilling its function to produce efficiently in two senses. First, efficient use of resources remains a relevant consideration, and must be somehow instantiated in the organization of the unit of production, if not as a profit motive, then as an analogous objective linked to productivity. Second, the unit must be efficient in the sense that what it produces satisfies wants. This means that the unit of production is concerned with demand. Both aspects of efficiency impose an external restriction on any internal decision-making process, whether democratic or not.

The same considerations confine the idea of collective governance of the economy on the macroeconomic level. At this level, collective determination of what is produced and how conflicts with both senses of efficiency, undermining productivity and impeding responsiveness of production to individual wants. The market remains, then, the primary institution for ensuring responsiveness of economic decisions to the demands of individual self-determination.

Indeed, democratic decision-making may have even less involvement in an economy appropriate to a democratic society, if by that we mean a society that assures adequate income to all citizens. In such a society, the connection between income and the sale of individual capacities (the labor market) is significantly attenuated, if not eliminated. This means that the need for macroeconomic policy directed at assuring full employment becomes considerably less urgent. It may also attenuate some of the need for government involvement in other policy areas so far as that need is implicitly or explicitly motivated by inequities in employment and income (see Schelling 1984).

Economic democracy

How does the matter of economic democracy appear from the standpoint of justice? The primary concern of justice is with individual self-determination, and with the regard for others it implies. Democracy, however, concerns group self-determination. The question of economic democracy, then, gets tangled up with that of the relation between individual and group.

Much depends on whether group ends displace those of the members, or represent and make explicit the universal aspect implicit members' ends. Is the group-constituting idea the universal selfhood of which the member is the particular? Or, is the group constituting idea a single common self that suppresses the particularity of the member? The governing idea of a democratic group is that the group does not suppress the autonomy of the member, but is constituted by the acting and willing of the members in a context conducive to the conscious emergence of the universal implicit in the life of the individual. In the first sense of a group, group rights and prerogatives do not take over from those of the individual, nor are group ends in conflict with the member's pursuit of self-interest.

Talk of economic democracy often points us toward questions of group rights; but the matter of workers' rights need not be about the group of workers. It can also be about the right of the individual worker to experience work in a way consistent with autonomy. Indeed, the call for greater economic democracy is often a call to make the organization of work conform better to expectations linked to individual self-determination: eliminating oppression, enhancing control of the work activity, and so on. We could, however, concern ourselves with matters such as this without making that concern into a call for greater democracy.

Indeed, we may wonder whether worker democracy necessarily enhances the integrity of the worker. Group self-determination may or may not enhance the self-feeling of the individual member. Much depends on the nature of the group, and on the degree to which it recognizes the end of individual self-determination. While we may hope that a democratically organized group will be more likely to recognize the autonomy of the individual, this is not inevitable.

The presumption that democracy will enhance autonomy, and thus secure a more just institutional setting, stems from the connection between democracy and justice. A democratic group is organized to respect the member's autonomy, since its decisions are the result of the autonomous willing of the members treated as separate persons; or at least they are so in principle. This is why democracy is a form of political process consistent with the demands of justice, and why justice often demands more democracy.

The danger arises, however, that, partly due to this connection, we might confuse justice with democracy, equating democratic outcome with what is just. This equation does not work precisely because it denies right its separate grounding in the idea of self-determination. So far as the ends of economic democracy are to eliminate oppression and enhance self-determination, especially through greater worker control over the experience of work, those ends are consistent with justice. Yet, while these ends may be consistent with justice, this does not mean that increasing economic democracy always enhances justice. Since democratizing the work place only places control into the hands of the group, it in no way assures that outcomes conform with the demands of justice.[31]

Justice implies reform of the work experience when that experience violates regard for personhood. Violation of the worker's right to a work experience consistent with personhood is not limited to settings in which the organization of production is privately owned, dedicated to profit-making, or publicly traded in the share market. Protection of right is equally the responsibility of the system of justice whether the enterprise is privately or publicly owned, or owned by those who work in it. Our problem is to understand better the demands justice makes on the organization of work, and not to circumvent the issue by invoking democratization, and then assuming that the democratic decision is always, or even defines what is, right.

Thinking this way tends to subsume the concerns usually associated with economic democracy under those of individual autonomy. This connection to autonomy can lead us to emphasize the extent to which the decision to undertake a particular kind of work expresses the worker's self-determination. That is, we might consider the organization of work consistent with worker self-determination if the worker enters that organization by choice, fully aware of its nature and implications. This might be the case if satisfaction of need or even want were not made contingent on the worker's accepting a wage contract offering conditions inconsistent with self-determination. The issue, once again, is that of the ability of society to generate enough wealth without making some undertake labor inconsistent with personhood. Those conditions that assure society this ability are the conditions within which the problems raised by those who demand greater economic democracy can be resolved.

The ends of individual and group self-determination

If we accept that rights have a grounding independent of democratic process, we must, as a matter of principle, protect rights from that process. In identifying rights, then, we distinguish two regions of society, one in which collective self-rule remains sovereign, another in which it does not. More specifically, if the economy is not and should not be democratic, the question remains concerning the appropriate terrain to be ceded to (non-democratic) economic processes within a democratic society.

Identifying the terrain on which democracy finds its home enables us to avoid being enmeshed in the confusions that result from organizing the problem of ethics and the economy around a dualism: participatory economy versus authoritarian economy. The just economy may be neither participatory nor authoritarian, since the authority within the economy may embody right. The problem is to understand when authority embodies, and when it violates, right.

One answer to this question refers us back to participation itself as the criterion for judging the legitimacy of authority (see Brenkert, 1992). This argument convinces us more the more we make participation the prime good to be achieved in the design of social institutions (see Dahl 1985). Doing so runs up against two difficulties of central importance. First it tends to devalue the end of individual self-determination in favor of the group. Claims legitimized by the will of the group as realized in democratic process do not override the claim of individual right, but, indeed, carry more weight the less the outcome can be argued on grounds of right. Second the argument for participation as the prime good begs the question noted above concerning the appropriate governance group.

Central to the questions raised by the discussion of needs and wants is the idea that we should protect and nurture a sphere of self-seeking not only for its own sake, but also as a 'root' (Hegel 1952) of the state as the embodiment of a public purpose. This idea implicates democratic institutions in a specific way. So far as democratic process makes demands on the autonomy and self-determination of citizens, demands that they decide for themselves and take responsibility for their political ends and actions, it assumes (and of course encourages) habits of mind consistent with autonomy. But, these habits of mind must be developed and nurtured outside of politics if they are to be well enough rooted to sustain a democratic political process. One primary place where the ways of life conducive to democratic habits of mind are nurtured is civil society.[32]

If we are unfree in society, if our livelihood has little to do with our self-determination, if our income is not our own, and if we cannot make meaningful decisions about work and consumption, then we can hardly be free in the political arena. Autonomy calls upon certain basic capacities and attainments, which, though differently expressed and exercised in different contexts, do not exist separately for those contexts. They exist, instead, as the animating principle of all institutions suited for subjective action. The more we politicize the economy, the more the sphere of autonomy shrinks and that of group determination expands, the more constricted the world of self-determination regarding work and ways of life, the less democratic is the seemingly democratic polity.

Capitalism and democracy

For some, capitalism and democracy embody the same principle: autonomy and the pursuit of individual self-interest. For others, they embody opposite principles: self-interest and the pursuit of group ends that transcend self interest. Since democracy roots group self-determination in the individual, it does not mark the limit of individual self-determination, but its realization in the context of group ends. Clearly, then, both capitalism and democracy raise individual self-determination to the level of a controlling force in shaping social institutions and processes. Because of this, the claim that each presupposes the other carries weight.

The difficulty is that both democracy and capitalism can also pose tangible threats to self-determination, and to a just society rooted in that principle, democracy because the will of the majority has no special link to respect for justice, and capitalism because it fosters hierarchies of personhood that encourage violation of autonomy, especially for those at the lower end (by degrading or exploiting them). This, then, poses a dilemma: two institutions rooted in the principle of individual self-determination, both of which endanger that principle.

One way to overcome this dilemma is to treat both capitalism and democracy in the context of social and economic development (see Pateman (1970). Then, the real end of democracy, like that of capitalism, is to liberate the principle of self-determination from the inhibitions and moral disapproval historically bound to it. The market economy plays a major role in doing so by providing the means for assuring each citizen an adequate measure of wealth, and by demanding that each citizen take responsibility for him or her self, thus making the self an inevitable and desirable end of thought and action.

Capitalism also expands and deepens the interdependence of persons. This theme of expanding interdependence, often associated with the division of labor, was an important one for Eighteenth and Nineteenth Century social thought. Adam Smith was among the first to insist on the growth of mutual dependence in production as a hallmark of a modern economy. Hegel picks up on this theme. He emphasizes how, in the pursuit of private ends, we are driven to seek out others and satisfy their needs so that they might be induced to assist us in the satisfaction of our own. Hegel sees this as the development of the universal in and through the particular. Marx carries further these classical themes. He characterizes capitalism as a system that overthrows the narrow parochialism of earlier society, destroys tradition, and disrupts personal dependence in favor of the impersonal connection of the 'cash nexus'.[33]

These changes, all associated with capitalist economic organization, create and further develop connections between persons based on universalistic considerations. They also bind the individual to an ever expanding system of interdependence. The idea of global interdependence expresses in contemporary language this same movement observed by philosophers, economists, and sociologists of the last century. This movement connects the particular (the individual part of the system of mutual dependence) to the universal (that system considered as a whole). While the self-understanding society develops under capitalism may impede the coming to awareness of the universal (especially in the form of public ends), capitalism still plays a prominent role in establishing social and economic organization on a more universal basis.

Democracy participates in the same development, although from a different direction. Democracy makes the collective the result of deliberation by the members who, while responsible to themselves as free citizens, must make that responsibility accord with the larger demands of a social order. By making each responsible for the whole, democracy simultaneously values the individual subject as end, and orients that subject toward collective and universal ideals. If this is correct, then, at least historically, there is a link between democracy and capitalism. They are two aspects of society's self-education in the value of the individual (and thus in the pursuit of subjective ends), and of the individual's education in his implicit social being.

Notes

1 The language Kohut (1977, pp. 134-5) favors carries this connotation.

2 Marx, for example, draws an important distinction between work and labor. In the following, I use the terms interchangeably.

3 This is the point emphasized by Arthur Okun (1975).

4 Most notably in the early modern period by Adam Smith and Karl Marx.

5 I discuss this idea further in Levine (1978, chapter 7).

6 Marx argues to the contrary that the demand for labor falls as capital increases. The analytic basis for this argument (that capital intensity increases more rapidly than capital) is not however established in his writings, nor is it very plausible.

7 This process has an international dimension that also needs to be taken into account. Lower paid jobs constitute a low wage sector within advanced economies, but are also allocated abroad to less developed economies with abundant low wage labor.

8 Actually, it will equal the sum of the subsistence and the inframarginal rent. Still, there will be no pool of profit to finance further expansion.

9 Ricardo refers to this as a distinction of the 'race' of workers.

10 Although an argument can be made for education as a public good, or, if not as a public good, as a good whose consumption creates sufficient externalities to warrant public involvement.

11 Except negatively, see Levine (1978, pp. 226-37).

12 Allen Wood (1972) interprets Marx's argument in this way, connecting it to Marx's theory of history and materialist critique of Hegel.

13 As one student of Marx points out, it is hard to think of a reason for using the term exploitation if not to imply injustice; see Cohen (1979).

14 For a fuller discussion see Levine (1998), Umari (1992), and Stirati (1994)

15 For a fuller discussion, see Levine (1998).

16 Adam Smith advances both of these ideas in *The Theory of Moral Sentiments* (Smith 1969). First, he emphasizes that what we want is to gain the esteem of others. This makes social being what we want, and regard for others a determinant of the content of wanting. Later, however, he insists on a conflict between reason and passion, and emphasizes the need for self-domination, by which he means (in part) that we must rule a self understood as a complex of passions that do not necessarily have interest in and regard for (universal) selfhood as their core.

17 There may be other reasons to attempt to make such goods private property. These reasons have to do with the incentive structure of a market economy, and with what we hope to accomplish by setting up incentives for persons in the way we do.

18 It need not, however, entail choice in the way that is interpreted in the so-called 'rational choice' literature, or in economic theory (see Levine 1998).

19 I use the term wealth here to refer to that part of the social product consisting of goods destined for consumption. If, instead, we equate wealth with the aggregate social product, then it includes

capital goods. In this essay, I do not consider explicitly a justice-centered argument regarding the rate and direction of capital investment.

20 Adam Smith makes the pursuit of esteem in the eyes of others the central motivating force that connects persons together into a system of interdependence. It plays a basic role in his understanding of the development of moral sentiments; see especially Smith (1969, pp. 203-9).

21 This would be reasonable and feasible assuming a capital stock adequate to the task of producing enough wealth to satisfy finite wants. Here again the question of capital accumulation becomes important.

22 For a fuller discussion of the matter of equality of distribution see Levine (1988) and Zucker (1995). In Levine (1988) the connection of inequality to justice emphasized here is not adequately considered, so justice is tied too sharply to equality of distribution.

23 We might wonder who is included in the 'all' referred to here. The answer is difficult, particularly in a global or international context. I return to these issues in Chapter 3.

24 In light of the difficulties bound up with use of the term equality (see Williams 1962) it may be better to formulate this point in other language, especially since the principle articulated is one of unequal distribution. We can say that equality of need satisfaction means that any need we satisfy for a member of our community must also be satisfied if it arises for another.

25 I explore this distinction in greater detail in Levine (1988, chapter 1).

26 There are other reasons why, in particular historical circumstances, growth may stagnate before either of these conditions has been met; see Baran and Sweezy (1966) and Levine (1978 and 1981).

27 Adam Smith does acknowledge the positive side of self-interest as end in itself and not mere means; see Smith (1969, pp. 283-93) and Hegel (1956, p. 38).

28 For a brief survey of the early history of these ideas see Khan (1974, chapter 1). On the role of recognition and quality of formative relations, see Winnicott on impingement (1960), Kohut on wholeness and fragmentation of self (1977), and Laing on the divided self (1965).

29 The relation between politics and economics is explored more fully in Caporaso and Levine (1992).

30 On these issues see Lindblom (1977) and Manzas (1992).

31 As eloquently pointed out by Hegel in a different context (1956, p. 43).

32 This is not the only place, since there is little hope for autonomy in civil society or politics if autonomy is not nurtured in the family.

33 In this connection, it is also worth mentioning Durkheim's distinction between mechanical and organic solidarity; see Durkheim (1984).

3 Global justice

Global justice

Introduction

At the beginning of this essay, I identified justice with the way we live with others, taking the term others in a strong sense that entailed real self-boundaries and the multiplication and differentiation of self into a world of many particular persons. This is a world of sameness and difference the unity of which is what we mean by other.

At that point in my discussion, I noted that many communities place others outside, thus disconnecting sameness from difference. Sameness is characteristic of members, difference of non-members. In such communities, to the extent that we need not live with others, justice is not a concern. The disruption of the unity of sameness and difference that challenges the dominion of justice is the central problem of global justice. Because, in a world of separate communities, sameness and difference are often placed apart, making sense of global justice poses significant difficulties.

Embedding justice

I have spoken of justice as an institutional embodiment of the ideal of living with others, where others refers not simply to an abstract difference, but to the specific construction associated with the idea of a separate self, the attainment of unit status, and the requirements, both internal and external, an individual must meet to be a 'center of initiative in the world'. Speaking this way makes justice a matter of laws and ideals. While this is important so far as it goes, it draws attention away from the ways of life that constitute the medium within which ideals and laws take root, or fail to do so. The rights and ideals we associate with justice flourish because they become embedded in the way people lead their lives. Life mainly goes on outside the institutions of justice, but this does not mean we can ignore ways of life when considering the prospects for social justice. The problem of the embeddedness of justice has special importance when we turn specifically to the matter of global justice.

If justice only really exists when embedded in the ways of life of a community, the emergence of global justice means the emergence of global community. For this global community to carry forward the idea of justice, it cannot be the mere aggregate of the separate national (and sub-national) communities. And, for justice to enter the spirit of the community, it must be more than the assertion (even on the part of a global legislative body) of abstract principles. Justice must be a living reality that begins in, and yet transcends, the particular (for example national) units whose higher aspirations it represents.

If, however, some communities arrange themselves around an idea of justice that others find alien, a tension develops, not only between communities, but within the language of justice. What is right locally may not be so globally. Living an ethical life as that takes on meaning for a local community may be unethical globally. But, making right wrong dislocates one of the primary values of community: its ability to provide its members with a feeling of security by validating the self-ideal instantiated in their ways of life.

If, for example, justice insists on freedom of religion, and even freedom from religion, it will find a religious community wanting. Members of that community, who orient their lives around the ideals of their religion, find themselves wanting in the eyes of an external justice alien to their community ideal. For that community, justice remains an abstraction, rather than a constitutive part of its way of life. Similarly, if justice demands an assurance of livelihood not provided by the market, then a community that organizes its economic life on the principle of laissez-faire fails to meet the standard of justice. Then, the idea of justice confronts the laissez-faire community as an external abstraction rather than constitutive part of its way of life.

Under circumstances such as these, justice challenges community not to live up to its own ideals, but to live up to ideals alien to, and subversive of, it. Yet, a meaningful appeal to justice seeks not to plant it in alien soil, or to disparage those who live differently, but to make its roots grow more firmly and deeply where it has already found its home. A finding of injustice has significance to the degree that the social arrangements of the community embody the principles of justice that have been violated. Where they do, injustice creates an obligation for the community and its members, the obligation to put right what is wrong. If it creates such an obligation, speaking of injustice is much more than moral posturing. It is a language in which a community secures its members and sustains its constituting values.

The considerations just advanced encourage us to ask questions about the universality of justice. Differences in judgment of what is right seem to suggest different notions of justice. If this is so, justice can only be universal if community is universal. Otherwise, justice is divided among communities, and particular to them. If justice is so-divided, it will take a universal community to make justice fully universal. Absent such a community, justice will remain imbued with the particularity of the community life that instantiates it. Yet, this particularity is not absolute. In the next sections, I explore aspects of the problem of the universal and particular in the idea of justice.

Tensions in ideas of justice

The two examples briefly introduced in the previous section highlight differences in concepts of justice, and in the organization of communities. Are these differences absolute? Do they make the notions of justice in one community irrelevant to communities where other notions prevail?

Differences in judgment of what is right may or may not imply that communities operate with disjoint and incommensurable notions of justice. This is because rights we deny might nonetheless be implicit in those we recognize. If the differences in rights between communities are differences in the degree to which certain rights are made explicit in different communities, then those differences are not absolute; and the judgments of right in one community are not irrelevant to other communities that deny all or some of the basis for those judgments.

Thus, for example, a community that organizes its economic affairs primarily through private transactions may deny its members any right to subsistence beyond that which follows from the right to use what property they have to acquire their subsistence if they can. Such a community does not take the right to livelihood as a component part of its idea of justice. This seems simple enough. Yet, the principle of private property and contract embodies the idea of respect for individual rights. Because it does, it has presuppositions and implications that go beyond the simple notion of ownership and use of things. It assumes that its members have the capacity to own and use, to recognize other's rights and the limits of their own. It also assumes the kind of knowledge and reason demanded by life in a system of private ownership. None of these assumptions can be met simply on the basis of natural capacities; each involves attainments that the community must facilitate in its members, for example by providing security or educational opportunity.

Facilitating the attainment of capacities is a basic need and might be a determinant of subsistence if we take subsistence to incorporate more explicitly the idea of security of the self emphasized above. Then, as a matter of justice, the public authority takes responsibility for securing subsistence, since only by doing so can it secure the member's capacity to enter into and participate in relations that embody the idea of justice, that is, relations of mutual regard and respect for difference. One of the most important of these relations is the contract for the transfer of property.

If a community oriented around property right ignores the conditions that make property real and meaningful to its members, it undermines one of its own foundations. Thus, we find the paradoxical result that communities organized around private ownership sometimes fail to secure respect for property among their members.

Clearly, one of the conditions that makes property meaningful to the individual is that he or she has a reasonable prospect of acquiring enough to gain a degree of self-satisfaction. Yet, arguments that appeal to individual initiative and self-determination are often used to support measures that make fulfilling this condition problematic. These arguments seek to minimize the mandate of government, and maximize that of the private sector. Maximizing the domain of the private sector makes want satisfaction contingent on property ownership, which tends to exclude those with little property from adequate satisfaction of want.

Beyond this result, minimizing government makes acquisition of the resources (e.g. education) needed to acquire property in and through the property system (market) also depend on property ownership, which places those without adequate resources in a double bind. As a result, their commitment to the property system tends to erode. Where the commitment of citizens to the idea of property erodes, this is likely to undermine the overall security of that system. Thus, once again, the more we institute the ideal of a pure private property system, the less secure will private property be. The more we are concerned to secure private property, the more our concern must be with its limits.

These considerations suggest that those members of the community who insist on a broader set of rights needed to secure respect for property, even though in conflict with stated and legislated rights, may better represent the community's spirit than existing law does. Indeed, establishing rights that limit the property system may be the only way to make that system secure. Those who seek to defend the property system against this extension of economic rights place that system at greater risk than do the critics of pure private enterprise. When more extensive economic rights are present in other communities, the judgments of others are not simply the judgment of those living in a different world, they are judgments that link up with the underlying ideals existing, even if only latently, in the community centered on property right.

This makes the matter of knowing when appeal to justice seeks to plant an idea in alien soil, and when it does not, difficult. We cannot judge the matter simply by referring to the stated and consciously known principles of community life. We must also know the implicit, sometimes disavowed, principles that underpin community life, and the contradictions in the community's ideals that mark the presence of opposed principles, and make relevant an appeal to seemingly unacceptable ideals.

Thus, a community that limits rights for certain of its members (women or minorities for example) creates a tension in that those excluded see themselves as lesser persons, which means they are and are not persons. To treat a person as something less is unjust. If this treatment takes place in a world where, outside the community, women or minorities are recognized as persons, this must strengthen the pole (of equality) that is disavowed in the life of the community. When the world community demands equality in a particular community that denies equality, it does not find the soil to be so alien as those seeking to preserve the community's traditional values might hope and expect.

Thus, the seeming differences in ideals of different communities may be less stark than they appear initially. If so, the prospects for global justice and global community will be brighter; and, the relevance of the demands global justice makes on the particular community will be greater.

Relativism of justice

The considerations just advanced call into question the notion of incommensurable ideals of justice in different communities, that is, of the relativism of justice. Some attempt to use the language of justice in a relativist sense, insisting that justice can refer to quite disparate, even conflicting, ideals. This relativism of the theorist encounters its opposite in the reality of justice existing within particular societies. In its embodiment within social institutions and social life, justice does not accept any notion that what it judges right and wrong is only contingently so. Indeed, justice, unlike its theorists, cannot itself be relativist.

Relativism undermines the aspirations of citizens to adopt ways of life embodying meaningful values when it impedes their efforts to treat those values as in a significant sense right. If conflicting values in other communities are also right, then citizens' ways of life are suspect not only to others but to themselves. Then, to adapt a phrase from a French philosopher, there is no right, there are only rights.[1] But, of course, no community could believe this and take what it deems to be right as only contingently so. If it did, it would inform its members that whatever they think is right is also wrong (that is, from some other 'standpoint'). For members to believe this, they must give up hope of knowing and living life according to what is good and right. They must, then, give up the hope of being good or right themselves.

Adherents of the relativist standpoint may not appreciate the serious consequences this erosion of the idea of right has for the mental life of the individual. The possibility of doing what is good or right has a fundamental significance. Good and bad, right and wrong are formative self-experiences that build into adult personality. To undermine the possibility of being good (or doing right) increases the danger of being bad (or doing wrong).

Psychically, to be good means to be worthy of connection, originally to the parent, later to the group.[2] Thus, the group can only exist by offering members the opportunity to have their goodness affirmed, and with it their sense of belonging. This offering binds the individual to the group. Relativism undermines this group constituting connection if it undermines the security the member feels in the judgment that he is good when he adheres to group values.

That our community values are particular might not matter if we live in isolation from communities with other values. But, once we live in contact with others, within an emerging global society, the issue of which is right cannot be avoided, as the relativist would hope (see Pleydell 1982). This means that one implication of the idea of global justice is that the truly universal aspect of justice can no longer be avoided. The universal aspect of justice makes claims of justice relevant where justice is only partially realized, or must share space with other conflicting ideals.

Justice and difference

The fact that communities deny that their ideas of justice are particular does not in itself overthrow the claim that justice is relative to community. Communities do differ significantly in the ways of life they deem just. How can we account for this difference without giving up the idea that justice not only codifies the demands of community, but also makes demands on community?

In order to answer this question, we need a way of distinguishing living with others from living in community. Living in community means pursuing a way of life consonant with the particular culture of that community, and may have, therefore, connotations consistent with relativist claims. Living with others, as I indicate above, places demands on conduct that transcend cultural particularity. The two are not always different and opposed; but, they may be. When they are, it means a division of the work of justice between integrating community and assuring that we respect others.

Indeed, when living in community does not entail living with others, justice, which insists on recognition of the other, can be corrosive of community. When integration means merger into a group, it means loss of self. It, then, opposes preservation of self in relation with another. When community seeks merger, it punishes difference. Integration of religious communities often attacks different ways of life not because they endanger others, but because they place self-determination above the arbitrary demands of community on members' ways of life. Justice made consistent with integration of such a community does not assure that we live with others, but punishes us when we are others. This is not justice as such, but justice with an admixture of its opposite. This admixture means something different than does the justice that protects us in our relations with others, and enables us to be other. Enabling us to be other means we can enter relations supported by justice that preserve difference.

Placing the other outside the community denies the connection between self and other. Denial of connection can, of course, be a powerful relationship in itself, which it is when we place others outside precisely in order to deny a real connection they have to us. Why do so? If those outside are others for us, their connection to our selfhood survives our denial of it. That is, we deny their selfhood not because they have no selves, but because of our need to disavow their selfhood. It makes sense for us to do so when those placed outside embody or represent aspects of our subjective life we cannot acknowledge and therefore integrate.

When others have this purpose for us, they are not simply different, but embodiments of a rejected community self. Then, others call forth fear and hostility.[3] Placing the other outside community implies a split in the community's psychic life that can foster relations of hostility between communities. When communities cannot integrate sameness and difference, but must place difference outside, this implies multiplication of communities, since each needs another to contain its denied self. The multiplication of communities on this basis means hostility between communities.

These implications of the splitting of sameness and difference have relevance for economics because they connect to the problem of exploitation. Connecting other to self negatively, as repository for its disavowed elements, can justify exploitation. We need not respect a selfhood in other whose existence we have denied. The demands of justice do not extend to our treatment of this denied other. Without the split between sameness and difference, the treatment of others we refer to as exploitation would be unjust. With that split, what would otherwise be exploitation becomes instead the appropriate use to be made of those who are not like us, who do not, or do not fully, embody selfhood, or embody only its negative aspects.

Splitting helps establish different orders of personhood. In a world structured around this difference, treating others as embodiments of selfhood would attribute selfhood to those the community does not acknowledge as persons. It is not unjust to treat non-selves, immature or inadequate selves, as unequal, with lesser rights, or without rights. If justice means giving each his due, the split of sameness and difference turns justice against itself by making it justify exploitation.

These considerations bear on an aspect of justice often emphasized in application of justice to economic affairs. This is the aspect of justice that calls for giving each member of a community what is due to him (or her), whether that be the regard due personhood in general, or, more concretely, the income due position, attainments, property, and so on.[4] This implies that justice entails respect for appropriate differences, and rejection of differential treatment where no relevant differences between persons are present.[5]

It might seem that the link between justice and dueness makes justice a matter of particular social and cultural practices, institutions, and values. This would, indeed, be the case if what is due cannot be determined without recourse to a prior specification of such practices, institutions, and values. Thus, as I suggest above, dueness justifies exploitation when difference is placed outside community. If, however, justice means living with others, and that means making otherness internal and acknowledged rather than external and disavowed, then dueness is amenable to an interpretation that embodies the universal we associate with justice.

What is due to others (those who are other to us in the sense employed above) is regard for their separateness as other persons, which is not contingent on cultural practice. Culture is relevant to justice because cultures may embody regard for others to different degrees. They may or may not respect and sustain the unity of sameness and difference referred to above as the self. What is due others as a matter of justice, however, is recognition of their sameness in difference, that is, that they are different selves. Each acts as a center of initiative; each knows and maintains self-boundaries; each pursues ends that incorporate the ideal of autonomy. Yet, each does so in his or her own way, pursues projects specific to him or her self, has interests, expectations, and life plans, uniquely his or her own. When this is the case, then each is a different self.

The problem lies in the relation between inequality and difference. If difference means difference in personhood (thus inequality), the sameness in difference is attenuated. If that sameness is not wholly obliterated however, then an element of equality of selfhood survives in the relation; and we can speak of justice even if its expectations are not fully met.

The sameness in difference, or selfhood of the other, cannot be wholly obliterated except by turning the other into an object. Doing so drains any residue of justice out of the relationship, since it eliminates the otherness necessary for any concern of justice to arise. Conversely, so long as the other is treated not simply as an object but as a person, even if a lesser person or even a person the property of another, justice will not be wholly irrelevant. Nor, however, will its demands be culturally specific, since they will connect to the element or residue of relating to other common to all matters of justice whatever the cultural milieu.

Justice and self-determination

Differences imply injustice when they impair our capacity for self-determination, or undermine our legitimate expectation to be treated with the regard due persons. For the individual, this involves respects self-boundaries and for the rights that sustain personhood. For the state, this involves a society of states that respects the self-determination and the sovereignty of each state (see Bull 1977).

For individuals, autonomy means determination of and by the self. As I argued earlier, the first condition that must be met for autonomy is the presence of a self. Some theories take this condition as axiomatic, perhaps thinking that not doing so questions the common humanity of all people by suggesting that some are and some are not selves. This axiom, however, obscures considerations vital to matters of justice and injustice. These are the considerations raised when we distinguish between the capacity or potential to develop an integrated core (or self), and the realization of that capacity or potential. It is one thing to question whether all, or virtually all, persons are born with the potential to develop the kind of core of personality we call a self. It is another to assume that having such a core presumes no specific developmental experience, and implies no specific social milieu.

Taking the potential for the reality drops all questions regarding the member's expectation that society will facilitate the transition from what could be to what is. Debates over social policy highlight the importance of this distinction. Such debates often pit those who believe that justice is served when discrimination on the basis of extraneous characteristics (race, ethnicity, gender) is excluded against those who believe that justice is only served when government assures that each citizen can develop his or her capabilities to their fullest. The latter standpoint insists that government act as a facilitator, and not simply to assure a level playing field.

The language of justice gets used in different senses, sometimes meaning to secure the rights of persons and sometimes meaning to secure the member's 'right' to become (so far as possible) fully a person. Treating the latter as a right connects the process to its end, but also confuses the two. The difference is important, as I will try to indicate further on.

For states, autonomy also has internal presuppositions centering on unification of the parts around a core. Recognition by other states depends on the capacity of the state to act as a coherent and enduring reality, to pursue projects, ideals, and ends that have an internal meaning. For this internal meaning to foster recognition of statehood, it must, of course, incorporate the general idea of what it means to be a state. This idea includes all that is entailed in a capacity to govern, to represent a community and its ideals, more specifically to represent a modern community with the ideals appropriate to it. These ideals include citizenship, with its unique connotations for the member and how he or she is viewed and treated by others and by the whole. While it is sometimes assumed that the formal presence of a politically constituted state implies that it possesses such a core, making this assumption confuses the substance of statehood with its form. However important the formal recognition of statehood, it only expresses or facilitates the emergence of the core of a real state.

In a modern community, right refers to the capacity for exercise of will that incorporates recognition of others, and justice to the system of (equal) rights, its elaboration, justification, and implementation. The notion of right conduct stems from the notion of an individual subject acting in a world of others equally so-recognized. Elevation of the subjective aspect connects justice explicitly to self-determination. In this world, injustice means deprivation of personhood, which means denial of self-determination.

Justice and the state

The natural domain for application of the concept of justice is the world of individuals relating to each other and to the state. Yet, the involvement of the state raises important questions. Do rights adhere to individuals qua individuals, or only as citizens of states?[6] Does other retain its sameness when we cross state borders? Or, does the unity in difference of self and other mean one thing within the state, another between states?[7]

The most obvious connection between rights and the state is in the area of enforcement. Yet, the state must have a reason to enforce rights, which it can only have if violation of right implicates more than the immediate parties concerned. To violate a right means to violate some individual's (or group's) right. But, this right only exists for the individual (or group) because it exists as such. To violate someone's right, then, also means to violate right. And violation of right is the concern of the community.

The state has a concern with right, then, because the state instantiates the ideal of right, an ideal that is threatened by violation of the rights of individual members. Then, a threat to the member's right is a threat to the whole, which must enforce rights in order to protect right. In this sense, the existence of justice depends on the state, just as the legitimacy of the state depends on the degree to which it instantiates justice.

Put another way, a community cannot exist wholly embedded in the everyday life of its members; it must also exist in and for itself.[8] How communities exist in and for themselves depends on the ideals they embody, and that are embodied in member's ways of life. In thinking about justice, and especially global justice, we need to think about the kind of institution adequate to represent the existence of a just community.

Such an institution must have the capacity to replace family and religious organization as representative and embodiment of the community taken as a whole. The need to replace family or church follows from the need to include others in community.[9] Traditionally, the state is understood, at least in principle, as the appropriate institution. Other institutions that might represent the whole -- church, clan, commune -- connect members in ways less sensitive to rights, and to the need to respect others, and include them in community.

If the state has this importance (in principle, if not always in practice), the concept of global justice, because it severs the link between justice and the state, faces a dilemma.[10] Severing the link between justice and the state severs the link between justice and community, since the state is the institutionalized existence of a community rooted in justice. The usual solution to this dilemma involves imagining a global state capable of incorporating right and justice, severed from any connection to particular nation, community, or culture. Yet, as many point out, this solution creates its own problems so long as national and cultural differences must be subsumed into global justice. If national or cultural difference stands in the way of the development of global society, a global state cannot be rooted in a global community.

The problem of the particular and the universal in the idea of the state has a practical solution in the development of the hegemony of one state in the state system. This one state is preeminent in wealth and power, a preeminence also tied to matters of ideology and culture. Hegemony has usually been considered from the standpoint of the problem of international conflict and the prospects for peace. Peace is important not only for itself, but also because of its implications for economic development. Thus, global peace under the leadership of a hegemon has been argued by some as a primary, if not the only, structure within which a trading system can develop conducive to economic growth.[11]

Hegemony also has a related significance in providing states with a self-ideal more universal than their own. The power and stature of the hegemon raises its self-ideal to a higher level. Even as that ideal incorporates values and ends peculiar to the culture and history of the hegemon, it also represents the guiding ideas of the state system as a whole, rising above the particularity of the self-ideals of subordinate states. This provides the state system with at least the rudiments of a universal self-ideal unavailable in the absence of the hegemon.

This solution, of course, raises problems precisely because of the peculiar unity of universal and particular the hegemon represents. That it is universal in important respects provides other states with an opportunity and dilemma, since it affords them the prospect of a public subject with a universal self-ideal, but also excludes them from acting as subject. As a result, they and their peoples are made the objects of the dominant state and its ideals. The dilemma is compounded, of course, to the degree that the hegemon represents its culturally particular self-ideal as the universal.

Global justice grounds rights outside the state, subordinates states to the demands of justice given without regard to their particularity, and raises individuality to a principle above citizenship and connection to particular community, particular nation. Global justice has difficulty with national particularity when cultural difference has ethical implications. Only if cultural differences, especially between states, are ethically neutral can they coexist with global justice.[12] Treating cultural differences as ethically neutral subsumes them into the same class, from the standpoint of considerations of justice, as individual differences. Aspects of our ways of life that individuate us need not make us greater or lesser persons, but can mark different life trajectories, each capable of realizing the ideal of personhood, if in different ways.

Cultural differences sometimes look very much like individual differences. Whether I favor rice or tortillas, opera or raga, African print or denim, need not rank me on a scale of good and bad, higher and lower. If cultural difference ends here, then it does not challenge justice. But cultural difference does not end here.[13]

Culture defines ways of life. In some cultures, the type of clothing appropriate to women hides them from public life and civil society. In doing so, it marks their restriction to the sphere of the family, excluding them from full citizenship. Similarly, housing arrangements, manner of greeting and recognition of others, forms of art, and so on can carry meaning relevant to matters of freedom and unfreedom.[14] When they do, the ways of life expressed can be subject to ethical judgment, though doing so is no easy matter.

To be sure, as Freud points out, we can invest otherwise trivial differences with substantial significance for personhood. In doing so, we make differences that, in themselves, have no ethical significance carry a burden of right and wrong. Then, those who are different in respect to the contingent elements of culture are judged harshly. When justice is embedded in culture, and defends not simply the ideal of self-determination and the separate or bounded self, it involves itself in this judgment of others. The justice that does so is a justice preoccupied with the solidarity constitutive of community, a justice that places the group or community above the individual, sacrificing the latter to group identity and communal ends.

One way of judging the justness of cultural differences considers differences just to the extent that they originate in self-determination. If we can be said to choose our different ways of life, the resulting differences would conform to the demands of justice. Using this criterion, we might seek to link the justness of differences in ways of life with access to alternatives. If we make this link, we implicitly connect justice to self-determined differences. If our way of life is not arbitrarily imposed on us, but follows our actions and decisions, if we are not arbitrarily excluded from ways of life available to others, then difference in ways of life (including difference in the wealth needed to sustain them) does not imply injustice.

The difficulty with this approach is that it can violate the integrity of culture and cultural difference. In a world where different cultures exist together, and at least tacitly offer themselves as options, the condition outlined above seems to demand that we be able to choose among cultures, that the culture of others must be available to us. But, can being a person mean choosing culture, or making our own personal culture? How can we integrate the idea of autonomy in finding our way of life with the necessity of cultural determination?

The modern answer to this question asks of cultures whether they adequately embody the principle of self-determination, or are built on hierarchy and the denial of personhood for at least some of their members. In other words, we ask to what degree is freedom instantiated in culture. If it is so-instantiated, then cultural determination is the path to self-determination. This approach takes seriously the link between global justice and self-determination. By doing so, it attacks the local ideals of justice embedded in societies for whom self-determination remains in some ways limited or implicit, and other values carry greater force.

Group self-ideals, then, are not simply a matter of contingent historical and cultural forms. While culture may give selfhood a special coloring and limit ways of life to what can be imagined under given historical conditions, cultural differences of this kind are not the important differences in group ideals. Rather, the vital differences have to do with the character of the relation of member to group, of individual to state. In this respect, the key element in the self-idea (or spirit) of the state is the way it integrates the member. True self-determination occupies a unique position along a spectrum of integration-separation. At either end of this spectrum lie real dangers to self-determination within community.

Ideals vary from those that make protection of the separate space of the member virtually the whole of the state's self-ideal to those that make loss of self into community the dominant pole. Thus, in the United States, separation is the rule, and little basis for integration of the citizen is established. By contrast, the Islamic state attacks separation, seeking to subsume the individual self into a communal identity and communal life. Each state represents for the other its opposing pole, a disavowed self that must be annihilated if the acknowledged self is to flourish.

The place of the self-ideal along the separation-integration spectrum has much to do with the limits the state places on the market and on the shape of market institutions. Political debate also has much to do with the struggle over the position the state occupies along the spectrum of integration-separation. In thinking about cultural differences between nations, we need to pay special attention to how these differences express different placement in the space of separation-integration.

Wealth and the commensurability of cultures

International differences in wealth allow citizens to use wealth to establish status in relation to citizens of other nations. Thus, the connection of wealth to hierarchies of personhood does not stop at national boundaries. Individuals can pursue wealth as a means to gain position in an (international) hierarchy of personhood. We can treat the amount of our national wealth as a measure of our worth, and thus implicitly of the worth of our way of life.[15] When we do so, we use wealth as a measure of worth for nations. This makes qualitative differences between ways of life quantitative. It also calls into question the idea that differences between national cultures make them incommensurable. The link between wealth and freedom makes wealth a relevant measure of culture.

A theorem implicit in economics, and emphasized above, holds that for culture to instantiate freedom it must afford the individual a measure of wealth adequate to develop a personalized way of life. This theorem expresses the link between freedom and the separation of persons (into distinct individuals).[16] The constitution of the individual self entails separation from others, which requires that the individual be able to afford a place distinctly his or her own. Establishing and marking such a place with objects appropriate to the individual requires the measure of wealth referred to here. Thus, freedom demands a measure of wealth, and poverty means unfreedom.

This idea lends credence to that of the commensurability of cultures. While the use of wealth to measure cultures seems not only arbitrary, but even in violation of respect for their basic qualitative differences, it also expresses the link between self-determination and wealth. We can use wealth to measure cultures in different ways. Some of these invoke a relation between ranking in a hierarchy of wealth and ranking in a hierarchy of personhood; others do not. While amount of wealth can be used to establish position in a hierarchy of worth, it can also be used to establish a relation to self-determination. The two uses, while often confused, are not the same.

Those cultures organized around the absence of adequate wealth to secure autonomy can be judged to fall short of those that have adequate wealth, just as those with adequate wealth that fail to use it to secure autonomy fall short of those that do. The precise amount of wealth needed for this purpose, and the unit in which wealth is measured, are, of course, historically contingent. This does not mean, however, that the ideal of autonomy is also contingent. If it is not, then we can argue that cultures are commensurable in the dimension of wealth because they incorporate, to different degrees, the conditions for autonomy.

How we judge this difference is another matter. Some insist that autonomy is a peculiar virtue to impose on cultures dedicated to other ends. We can, of course, use autonomy as the basis, through wealth, for establishing a commensurability of cultures whether we agree with this assessment or not. Our assessment of the virtue of autonomy, and its place implicit or explicit in different cultures, then determines the significance of the measure.

The connection between wealth and freedom makes sense of the use of wealth as a measure of the degree to which a nation or culture has achieved self-determination as a whole and for its members. This does not imply that more wealth always means more freedom, or that to live in wealthy society is to be free. While the use of wealth to make cultural differences commensurable expresses a fundamental truth about cultures, it does not say all we can about the differences between them. Still, from the standpoint of wealth and what wealth signifies, cultures are commensurable. We ignore something important about the aspirations common to cultures when we disparage the use of wealth to measure their success.

In light of the use of wealth to establish commensurability of cultures, it is not surprising to find a connection between wealth and hegemony. Not only does wealth facilitate the coercion that establishes hegemony, it also underwrites claims that the culture of the hegemon is a higher culture, one which others will do well to emulate. If greater wealth facilitates a greater measure of freedom, at least for some and possibly for many, then hegemony derives from self-determination. The hegemon is not only self-determining because it dominates over others, it dominates over others because they recognize its greater capacity for self-determination. Since the relations between the hegemon and other states incorporate domination and subordination, they do not realize global freedom, but in important respects conflict with it. Nonetheless, the existence of a hegemon indicates the role self-determination plays in structuring a system of domination.

International inequality

Inequality

Inequality of income and wealth is a kind of difference between persons and between states. It is a difference that bears on the matter of justice when it implies that having less income and wealth entails violation of personhood, or calls into question the sovereignty of the state. If inequality means that many live in poverty, then it has a special bearing on the justice of social arrangements.

Poverty limits opportunities for self-expression, creates insecurity, undermines physical capacities bound up with being fully a person, limits educational opportunities, and so on. We might say that poverty deprives the individual of certain prerequisites of autonomy. Thus the state of poverty is one where justice is not realized. Yet saying this need not imply that anyone, or that any group, has deprived the poor of their personhood, or otherwise undermined their autonomy. Injustice, then, differs from the state of a society that is not fully just.

If we acquire our wealth with due regard for the rights of others, and we acquire an amount different from theirs, this difference does not imply that we are responsible for injustice. But, if we acquire our wealth by depriving others of theirs, or otherwise use wealth to deprive them of due regard, the resulting inequality implies injustice. That inequality is not unjust does not, however, make it right. We have to consider not only the possibility of injustice, but also of the absence of justice, or that justice is only partially realized.

It can be difficult to know when differences in wealth imply injustice, and when they do not. The difficulty arises because of complexities in the idea of what is due a person in the area of income and property. Some argue that inequality is not unjust so long as it does not arise unjustly, by the expropriation of the property of others. Yet, knowing when this is or is not the case can pose some significant difficulties.

Inequalities arising from self-determined differences in the use of rightfully owned wealth incorporate the justness of the original endowments, and of the process by which they gave way to the new. If this is the case, and that process has the potential to foster the development of dramatic inequalities, even poverty for some, then, on this argument, we are forced to conclude that those inequalities are also just, even though they might undermine the idea of common personhood, and impede the prospects for equal opportunity, for the poor or across generations.

This approach to the problem, though simple in principle, clearly raises intractable difficulties if it demands that we establish a just initial endowment. The justness of any current distribution is contingent on the justness of the original endowments out of which that distribution arises. Yet, asking that initial endowments be just conflicts essentially with the whole notion of development. As i suggest in the next section, development is, by nature, a process in which the characteristics of the end are only latent in, and in many ways violated by, the process of realizing that end. We cannot, then, expect the development of justice as an end to be a just process. Logically speaking, then, we cannot expect to reconcile the procedural notion of justice with any meaningful notion of justice as the end of a process of development. If we consider justice in purely procedural terms, then it either exists or does not. Thinking this way denies that justice is embedded in society, and that society and social institutions must achieve a level of development consistent with the demands of justice.

The conflict between justice as a procedure for distributing wealth, and justice as an attribute of the outcome of that procedure, is a real one. It arises not because of inadequacies in the concept of justice, but because of attributes of the world in which the pursuit of wealth as an end turns a just procedure into an unjust outcome. In a world oriented around wealth accumulation, we face a choice between the two poles of justice: procedural and end state. But, neither choice works well. Choosing the justice of an end state makes justice ephemeral, as one critic forcefully argues (Nozick 1974). Yet, choosing the justice of procedure, as that same critic favors, ignores implications for justice of the results of application of those procedures in the context of wealth accumulation.

The search for justice in distribution naturally encounters this sort of conundrum. Insisting that right be respected in the procedures by which income and wealth differences emerge should assure that those differences are consistent with justice. But, no procedure can respect right when the conditions demanded by justice have not been met, particularly the condition that we can produce enough wealth without violating the integrity of its producers. Here, again, the matter of the embeddedness of justice cannot be ignored. We cannot meaningfully speak of justice in abstraction from those conditions of living needed to make justice real, as theories of justice often attempt to do.

Poverty and exploitation

Poverty means deprivation and dependence. This implies a link between poverty and characteristics of psychic and group life that result from failure of autonomy. To be poor means to lack vital requisites for self-determination, beginning with wealth. The idea of fate fits this condition well, since both fate and poverty deny self-determination. Without a sense of autonomy, the member lives in his or her world as object rather than subject. Fate incorporates this idea about the relation of member to world. While this may not imply exploitation, fate as an organizing principle for a way of life facilitates exploitation.

Exploitation refers to our use of others as means to our ends, often ends involving acquisition of wealth, without due regard for their personhood. By using others in this way, we debase them as persons. To exploit someone is wrongfully to claim the product of his or her labor, talent, ingenuity. To charge exploitation is to invoke an idea of right. Invoking an idea of right places us in the context of ethical judgment, which presumes an ethical community, and an idea of justice.

Poverty normally feeds exploitation, since the poor are vulnerable to being used by those who are not poor, or are less poor. This connection between poverty and exploitation suggests that we should not expect to find justice realized in the context of widespread poverty. If the need to exploit others is strong enough, that need can be a force creating or sustaining poverty. In other words, economic arrangements can assure the provision of a supply of the poor adequate to underwrite exploitation. Marx emphasizes the necessity of maintaining poverty as a condition for exploitation. He attempts to demonstrate that the process of capital accumulation displaces workers and increases what he calls the 'reserve army of the unemployed'. This reserve army presses the wage of the employed worker down to the subsistence level, assuring one necessary condition for exploitation. The causal relation between poverty and exploitation is now reversed, since the former arises because of the demands of the latter.

If we insist that livelihood must depend on exchange; if we deprive the poor of a safety net of welfare measures that can secure a way of life conducive to the gaining of skills necessary to making an adequate living; if we deprive children of adequate food, shelter, safety, and education, then we assure the reproduction of poverty from generation to generation. Assuring the reproduction of poverty assures that our society will fall short of meeting the requirements of justice. It will also assure the reproduction of a population susceptible to exploitation.

International exploitation

In a global system where some nations are poor, the principle of justice is not fully realized. In such a system, a question arises concerning the responsibility of the wealthier nations for global poverty. To address this question, we need to determine the relation between poverty and wealth accumulation. In particular, we need to consider how the mechanisms of accumulation do or do not lead to impoverishment.

One of the most important of these mechanisms is competition. In competition over markets, income and wealth grow for some, not for others. Competition can lead to impoverishment, as when Japanese competition adversely affects employment and incomes of Detroit auto workers. Such effects of competition should be clearly distinguished from those of expropriation and exploitation. When the British forcibly bring about the destruction of the Indian textile industry in order to open up a market for British textile producers, the accumulation of wealth in England is causally linked to the impoverishment of India not by competitive advantage, but by expropriation. Forcible expropriation of markets may be unjust in itself. But beyond this, it can also prepare the ground for exploitation.

Some seek to subsume competition into exploitation. They argue that, even in a free market without government intervention, an international transfer of wealth takes place through unequal exchange or the transfer of profit made on foreign investments in poor countries. This use of the term exploitation, while analytically different from Marx's, carries a similar meaning: a market based on legally free contract can bring about a transfer of wealth from those who in some sense produce it to others who become rich by acquiring it.

This argument runs into difficulty in Marx's original formulation because Marx does not clearly link his use of the term exploitation to a concept of social justice.[17] Indeed, Marx insists that, so far as one cares to pursue the matter, the capitalists who benefit from exploitation have the 'right' to do so (see Wood 1972). Marx never makes it clear how we are to understand exploitation when it does not mean violation of right.[18] Nonetheless, Marx evidently has an implicit claim in mind that since workers produce the wealth, they retain some compelling right to it, even though legally this right is not recognized.

A similar difficulty arises in the effort to treat competitive disadvantage as a matter of injustice when that disadvantage is not imposed by political, military, or other means clearly in violation of rights (such as the nation's right to self-determination). We could, of course, assume that inequality must imply injustice, thereby making the result of competition unjust by definition. We might do so either because we think that inequality is always and inherently unjust in itself, or because we think it is always (or virtually always) a result of injustice, even when we have difficulty pinpointing the particular injustice that brought about the inequality.

If we follow the first of these two lines of reasoning, we understand justice as an outcome: equality in access to wealth and income. As I suggest above, an argument can be made in favor of such an interpretation of justice, particularly where differences in wealth and income establish hierarchies of personhood. But, having justice demand equality weakens its ability to defend the differences between persons. If defense of equality is our goal, it would be better to do so on grounds other than justice, as Marx seems to do when he treats justice as a part of the prevailing institutions of exploitation. The alternative is to treat differences in income not as unjust in themselves, but as unjust only when they result from or imply violation of personhood. Only if competition inherently violates personhood would its result be inherently unjust. If it does not, then, we need to maintain a clear distinction between exploitation and competition so that we can evaluate their separate implications for injustice and the responsibility of the rich for the condition of the poor.

Given these considerations, how might the market mechanism bring about the exploitation of some for the benefit of others? When can we judge the outcome of the workings of the property system unjust in this sense? The attempt to find exploitation in the workings of the market runs into difficulty because of the market's grounding in the principle of quid pro quo. The idea of the market as a set of voluntary transactions implies that, in the judgment of participants, exchange yields an improvement in welfare, since, if it did not, one or the other party would refuse to participate. By its own measure of value, a market transaction, entered into with reasonable knowledge and without coercion, cannot lead to the gaining of wealth by some at the expense of others.

Marx suggests two ways to circumvent this impediment to linking markets and exploitation. One challenges the assumption that market exchanges are voluntary transactions. That they are legally uncoerced need not mean that they are so substantively. Much depends on the options available to the parties. If, for one party, the options are too narrow, that party has a disadvantage in the transaction that could call into question its voluntary nature.

The classic example of disadvantage in this sense is the labor contract (see Lindblom 1977). Since Adam Smith, economists have noted how the labor contract favors the purchaser, whose urgency to contract is less, and whose options are greater. The worker, whose livelihood is at stake, may therefore be coerced by circumstance, if not by the buyer of his or her laboring capacity. Coercion, even of circumstance, undermines any claim that the outcome of the contract is (substantively) voluntary and therefore just.

Coercion of this kind is not, of course, bound by national borders, but can develop wherever wealth faces poverty, and the poor have few options (see Beitz 1985). In this, the international setting is of no special consequence except that the potential exists there for the state to prevent exploitation of the poor within its borders. But, the poor are more than likely citizens of poor states, and poor states often have limited capacities and will to protect their citizens. If, as a result, their policies are skewed against the interests of domestic economic development, and in favor of foreign investors or foreign states, then we can say that their poverty begets exploitation at the hands of the wealthy.

We can also say that it is the state that must prevent exploitation, as it is the absence of a strong state that opens the door to exploitation. This is, in its way, true more generally. What stands in the way of exploitation is the presence of a subject capable of establishing and defending self-boundaries, whether that subject be individual or collective. Since it is only through the state that the community can establish itself as a subject, it is only through the state that it can secure its integrity and prevent exploitation by those outside.

Preventing international exploitation is, then, a matter of state development. State development requires both external and internal conditions conducive to it. That is, a strong state might fail to develop because the state system impedes that development, for example because a hegemon blocks the emergence of a political order it sees as a threat to its power. A strong state might also fail to develop for internal reasons having to do with political and social structures inconsistent with the integration demanded for a strong state to emerge (see Geertz 1963).

Marx's second suggestion for linking exploitation with free markets is that we not take at face value the market evaluation of the properties exchanged. In markets, money buys goods and at the same time measures their value (Marx would say their exchange-value). If this money measure is the only way we can know the value of goods, then, by definition, exchange is a relation of equality both in form and substance. But, if the money measure hides a different underlying measure of value, the possibility arises that the trading of goods at their market prices may be an exchange in which one party gains value at the expense of the other.

Theorists seeking to find exploitation in the working of the global market system appeal to this line of argument, and particularly to the labor theory of value used by Marx to demonstrate that exploitation is the hidden reality of quid pro quo. In their arguments, an exchange of equivalents as measured in money will simultaneously be an unequal exchange of value when measured in labor embodied. Unequal exchange transfers wealth from one party to another, possibly from those in poor nations to those in rich ones. When this happens, the rich become so at the expense of, therefore through exploiting, the poor.

The argument centered around unequal exchange makes the state complicit in exploitation, rather than a defense against it. So far as the state sustains free market economic institutions, it allows some to exploit others, and can be considered responsible for the exploitation visited on part of its population. This is true, of course, only so far as the argument centered around unequal exchange carries weight.

This line of argument runs into several difficulties, beginning with those associated with ambiguities in the labor measure of value, and with its weak underpinnings in a theory of justice. The distribution of rights in relation to valuation is not well established, nor are we clear why labor is an appropriate measure of value, or why unequal exchange of labor violates right (and therefore implies exploitation). It is also unclear that the accumulation of wealth depends in any significant way on the transfer of wealth from poor to rich. This latter would seem an implausible claim, since it suggests we look to poverty as the source of wealth (see Lewis 1978).

If we reject the charge of exploitation, this does not commit us to a favorable or benevolent judgment of global differences in wealth. As I have argued elsewhere, the global economy is a powerful force for uneven development (Levine 1982). This is primarily because accumulation of capital and wealth follow competition over markets and market shares. Indeed, competition is the primary mechanism of accumulation, which means that the process of growth and development is one that can result in poles of wealth and poverty. This does not mean, however, that the wealthy become so by appropriating the wealth or surplus of the poor. On the contrary, they become wealthy by appropriating more than their (domestic) share of the global market. They accomplish this by a combination of means including, but not limited to, the violation of the sovereignty of their competitors. Indeed, the logic of the process compels the conclusion that the result would happen (although winners and losers might differ) with or without such violations of sovereignty. The more we emphasize the role of markets in the accumulation process, the more we diminish the importance of the poor to that process since, after all, the one thing the poor cannot do for the rich is buy the goods they need to sell to become and remain rich. The tragedy of global poverty may have more to do with this irrelevance of the poor than with their exploitation as a way to produce wealth.

As a general rule, when some become wealthy, others do not. But, violation of rights in the process by which the differences in wealth arise is not the essence of the matter. Whether the outcome is unjust, then, depends on whether we define the justness of wealth differences according to outcomes, or to the process leading to those outcomes. Is global inequality inherently unjust, or only when it results from the violation of rights (other than a supposed right to equal amounts of wealth)?

I suggest above that the answer to this question depends on whether wants are finite, and whether there is enough wealth to satisfy those finite wants. When there is enough wealth to satisfy (finite) want, justice will not be served by equality of income. Where there is not sufficient wealth and wants are not finite, the conditions for justice are not satisfied and application of its criteria will certainly lead in conflicting directions (for example by supporting both equality and inequality). In this regard, perhaps Marx was correct in thinking that injustice is not a powerful concept for dealing with the impact of capital accumulation on the human condition. Marx does not celebrate the ethical virtues of capitalism; but, he does see it as a part of the process of development necessary to bring into being a social order that does exhibit those virtues, a world in which the many sided development of all individuals is the real end of social arrangements. Marx sharply, perhaps too sharply, distinguishes the end from the process of its development, a distinction that those who employ the language of justice to judge social arrangements might do well to consider more seriously.

Does this mean that wealthy nations have no responsibility for global poverty? The answer is obviously complex, since it calls on our knowledge of what relationships and policies foster or impede development. Thus, for those who believe that free market policies foster development, noting that wealthy nations encourage or even impose those policies on developing countries is an instance of encouraging development toward a situation conducive to realizing justice. For those who believe that free market policies impede development, encouraging of imposing such policies impedes the development of conditions necessary for realizing justice. The same issue can be raised about the whole range of policies that link developed and less developed nations. Since the issue is the development of the conditions in which justice can be realized, and not the immediate realization of justice without regard to those conditions, the question is not about justice as such, but about justice as an end to be accomplished by means that, since they cannot assume justice as a precondition, must in some ways fail the test of justice.

The limits of distributive justice

The difficulty we have in speaking of exploitation as a dominant force in shaping the global political economy mirrors the difficulty we noted earlier in speaking of distributive justice. Making justice bear on income distribution has meant seeking justice under conditions of scarcity. Doing so assumes that justice can be achieved where there is not sufficient wealth to satisfy want. Seeking to achieve distributive justice, then, makes justice depend on conditions that may be inconsistent with the ideal justice represents. This problem with arguments concerning distributive justice has been a main theme of the foregoing discussion.

As I emphasize above, wealth may be insufficient to satisfy want for two reasons. First, the link between wealth and worth provides a quantitative measure of self-esteem assuring that no amount of wealth will ever be enough. Second, capital accumulation may not have proceeded to the point where enough wealth can be produced to satisfy even discrete and finite wants. The pursuit of global justice runs up against both of these problems. Countries that have a sufficient industrial base to satisfy domestic wants may be impaired in their ability to do so because their economic well-being depends on the continuing accumulation of capital. Dependence of well-being on growth is typical of capitalist economic organization, as all the classical economists observe.

In a capitalist economy, production takes place as a means to the expansion of wealth. Since expansion is the reason for production, well-being depends not simply on the existing productive capacity, but on prospects for its increase. A capitalist economy is not a system of reproduction, but one that either expands or stagnates.[19] This quality makes even developed economies vulnerable. Development cannot assure that wants will be satisfied even so far as they could be given existing productive capacity.

An important arena of vulnerability is the global economy, especially for states that follow a policy of openness (see Levine 1995). Competing in the global economy forces countries to pursue continued expansion of their share of global markets, since the alternative is relative impoverishment through loss of markets, income, and employment abroad. For the developed countries, then, openness of markets and participation in a global system of competition over markets means that no amount of capital and wealth can be enough.

It also means that competition from developed countries continues to pose a threat to economic growth in the less developed. Less developed countries do not have a capacity to produce wealth adequate to meet the needs of their citizens. Their problem is not simply one of achieving justice by satisfying wants, but of developing their capacity to satisfy wants to the point where justice could be achieved. To the extent that competition from abroad impairs this development, openness to the global economy can impede movement toward laying the foundation for economic justice at home. Achieving global justice may require, then, limitations on global competition. Such limitations would allow less developed countries a better opportunity to develop the industrial infrastructure needed to produce enough wealth to secure domestic justice. It would also allow the developed countries to pursue ends, possibly connected to economic justice, inconsistent with continuing pursuit of a dominant position in a system of global competition.

It cannot be assumed, however, that restructuring the global system will in itself assure the conditions for justice in poorer countries. Assuming that it will assumes that the only real impediments to economic development and justice are external, and that the poor are poor only because others have made them so. But, however important the structure of the global political economy to the plight of the poor, it should not be allowed to distract us from the internal conditions that create and recreate poverty.

The difference is not only between opportunity and the capacity to take advantage of opportunity, it is also between what I refer to above as the rights of persons and the right to become a person. The idea that we have a right to become a person suggests that the process is one that happens at our will. This assumes that we will ourselves to become persons just as persons will the use of their property or how they vote in elections. But, to be not yet fully a person, as is implied in the right to become a person, is to be impaired in precisely that capacity associated with the exercise of right: will, and the self-determination it presumes. Thus, we cannot have a right to become a person, and the part played by right in our development into the bearer of right must be considered a special problem in itself: the problem of development.

The idea of development poses special problems for justice, which promotes development when it is identified with universal rights, yet can impede development when identified with the process by which a community institutes whatever norms it takes to be definitive. In the latter case, justice is relative to community, and, therefore, cannot support any development with which the community's norms are not consistent.

Notes

1 'There is no reason, only reasons,' Jean-Francois Lyotard quoted in Yeatman (1994, p. 106).

2 For a full discussion, see Fairbairn (1952).

3 For further discussion, see Pleydell (1982, pp. 168-71) and Volkan (1988).
4 On justice as dueness, see Miller (1976) and Zucker (1995).
5 This connects dueness to the impartiality emphasized by Ginsberg (1965).
6 Even if, as Ronald Dworkin (1977) argues, we have rights against the state, this does not mean that our conception of justice does not include the state.
7 These issues are explored in Beitz (1985) who goes so far as to argue that growing economic interdependence has made the state-centered image of the world lose its 'normative relevance' (p. 305).
8 This aspect of the state is not much emphasized in recent literature due to the increasing influence of utilitarian, contractarian, and Marxian ideas that tend to view the state as a mechanism or instrument of interests. For treatment of the substantive ends of the state, particularly those linked to making the whole an objective reality, see Hegel (1952) and Durkheim (1958).
9 Critics of so-called state centric approaches need to show how we can have justice without the state, rights without right, a just community that exists only embedded in the particular lives of members and not in itself. Further, they need to show how the institutions of justice can carry moral force if they are solely institutions of enforcement of right and do not also develop right into an objective collective reality.
10 The problems that arise here are familiar in international relations theory, which concerns itself with whether a society of states can be an ethical order; see Bull (1977), Nardin (1983), and Walker (1993, chapter 3).
11 This aspect of hegemony has recently been given special emphasis; see Kindleberger (1973), Keohane (1984), and Strange (1987).
12 For a fuller discussion of neutrality of cultural difference, see Blaney (1994).
13 See Dewey (1939, pp. 9-10).
14 Hegel (1956, pp. 69-70) points this out with regard to the distinction between form and subject-matter in art.
15 For a relevant discussion see Blaney and Inayatullah (forthcoming).
16 See Hegel's discussion of the multiplication of needs (Hegel 1951).
17 It also runs into difficulty because of its dependence on a theory of how wealth is produced that attempts to connect the amount of value produced to the labor expended.
18 Allen Wood's effort to solve this problem by separating servitude from injustice captures much of the spirit of Marx's method (Wood 1972). This narrows the concept of justice to a purely legal category and, in doing so, creates serious problems. Servitude itself must be

considered in some sense wrong, and the sense of wrong we attach to servitude will surely bring into play considerations of autonomy, integrity, and self-determination difficult to separate from the idea of justice.

19 This point is first fully developed by Marx in (1967). For more recent discussion, see Baran (1957), Baran and Sweezy (1966), and Heilbroner (1985).

4 Justice and development

Capitalism's historical mission

The most difficult practical problems for justice arise not in maintaining a well established system of justice consistent with its ideals, but in the emergence of justice where it does not exist, or exists only latently. To cope with the practical concerns of justice, then, we need something more than a concept of justice as a norm realized to a greater or lesser degree in prevailing institutions. We also need an understanding of the process (development) that, because it makes justice an end, cannot be just in itself. As I suggest above, that persons have rights does not in any simple way imply a right to become a person, nor does it imply any other simple solution to the problem of the role of justice in the process of its own development.

Marx understands this point. He formulates his critique of capitalism around what he calls its 'historical mission'. This mission is to create the material base for what Adam Smith refers to as 'civilized society'. The society Marx envisions arising on this foundation differs radically, perhaps too radically, from the society he deems well suited to the construction process. In many ways, Marx's version of civilized society is the antithesis of the society required to lay its foundation. Still, Marx understands that the process that creates civilized society cannot be all that civilized.[1]

The reason Marx constructs the end of the process as its antithesis has to do with the way he understands self-interest. Marx identifies self-interest with the self-aggrandizing pursuit of the capitalist. In the worst case, which Marx also finds typical, this means exploitation of others. The strong link between self-interest and exploitation means that a civilized society must be one that overcomes self-interest.

The socialist experiment of the twentieth century was rooted in the idea that economic development could take place on the basis of motivations other than self-interest, in particular the sacrifice of the individual to the group. The failure of the experiment revealed a failure in this premise. What the socialist experiment attempted was to sever the link between interest in the self on one side, and the process that lays a foundation for a just society on the other. In the language developed earlier, it made interest in the self inconsistent with interest in the group. This meant, of course, that (individual) self-determination could not be central to the group ideal. In light of this exclusion, it is not surprising to find social arrangements that give little room for development of individuality, with the implied eclipse of civil society. Here, the particular self is viewed as a danger to the collective (or universal) self, with damaging consequences on both levels.

In effect, the socialist experiment attempted to sever the connection between justice and autonomy. Yet, an important benefit of (economic) development lies in the access wealth provides to a new way of life rooted in individual autonomy, and in the validation of the self as an end. The end of development is a just society, if by that we mean one where autonomy is secured by wealth. If this is so, there is more of justice in the development process than the access to wealth it ultimately provides. This something more is contained in the part self-interest plays as its moving force (see Hegel 1956, p. 38).

Nothing can appear as a result that does not exist in its process of becoming. Development cannot simply be the process that creates a material foundation for its antithesis: a civilized life. Development must also be the process of learning what it means to lead such a life. Since capitalism is the organization of society around the process of development, capitalism cannot be simply the antithesis of civilized society, but must contain the new form of civilization within it, a new form that emerges progressively with the advance of the process of capitalist development itself. Thus, so far as we follow Marx in thinking that capitalism is part of the development process, we must conclude that its institutions and their outcomes are not just. At the same time, so far as we follow this line of thinking, we must conclude that justice is nonetheless latent within, and importantly a part of, capitalist economic and social organization.

Marx emphasizes this last point, but only on a narrow basis. Aside from abstract and isolated allusions to the many sided development of man, Marx focuses attention on the technical rather than social and individual foundation for a civilized society set by capitalist development.[2] Marx emphasizes the role of capitalism in setting a material foundation for a real development of the individual, while blocking the result for which the foundation has been set. In his later work, Marx tends to sacrifice the idea of the development of the individual, seeing in the emergence of cooperative forms of production, and in the levelling of workers' conditions, the mark of a new society that overcomes individual difference.

Yet, the emergence of a new order cannot be so easily severed from the emergence of self-determination as its guiding principle. Self-determination does not exist fully formed from the outset, but develops through its own process. It is important that the pursuit of self is the guiding principle of capitalism, and in this establishes capitalism as a vital part of the development of justice; and it is important to understand the limitations of the self whose pursuit capitalism fosters. This means that the pursuit of self we find typical in the earlier stages of development is not the same pursuit, nor is its object the same self, we expect to find at the end. The difference between the two is vitally important to matters of global justice and economic development. It helps us understand how pursuit of self-interest can impede justice, even though self-determination is justice's end.

Moments of the development of the self

Development is the simultaneous presence and absence of an end. The development with which we are concerned here is that of the self: of self-interest, self-determination, and self-feeling. To understand this development, we need, then, a clearer understanding of the self, and of the moments of its development. With this clearer understanding, we can see how the self is both part of the development process, and also the end of development. This clearer understanding would allow us to distinguish moments of the self, and thus see it as both present and absent.

One way to consider the self both present and absent draws on the dialectic of self-alienation and self-integration.[3] The self in its development process exists in a state of alienation from itself. The end of that process is, then, the state of self-integration. The notion of self-alienation suggests that the self is divided in some way, and that parts or aspects are disconnected (disavowed, disassociated) from it. It remains to be seen, however, in what respect the self is divided. To begin to conceive the self divided, and therefore to see its development as a movement from alienation to integration, we must give up the idea of the self as a simple, one dimensional, entity: a simple locus of desire, or of unitary longing. To think of the self as the object of development means that we cannot take it for granted, but must consider it a structure shaped by a formative process.

When we think of the self as a complex entity or structure, we see it as a unity of distinct parts or aspects. These parts or aspects are the self's capacities: the capacity to think, act, and will; the capacity to separate or differentiate from others; and the capacity to recognize self in other. The self is also a way of organizing and connecting its capacities into a unit: Do the capacities work together in the attainment of consistent goals; or, does the exercise of one preclude the exercise of others?

Of special relevance to political economy are the capacities to separate from, and recognize the self in, others. Above, I refer to the aspects of the self linked to these capacities as the particular and universal. To establish self-boundaries, to separate and individuate, makes the self something particular, even unique. To recognize its own selfhood in others, who are also particular and unique individuals, makes the self something universal, shared with other selves. Self-integration means the unity of these two aspects of being a self. Self-alienation means the sacrifice of one to the other, so that the self cannot establish its uniqueness without rejecting the existence of other, different, selves; or, it gives up its individuality to join with others in a shared selfhood of the group or community.

Especially relevant for matters bearing on economic justice is the splitting off of the self's purely particular, narrowly self-referential, aspect. This is the aspect or moment of the self that capitalist economic organization confuses for the whole. By fostering it, capitalism fosters the development of the self; and by fostering it, capitalism impedes the full development of an integrated selfhood, which is a selfhood that combines both its particular and universal aspects.

The isolation of the particular dimension of selfhood, and the interpretation of what is particular about a self as the whole of what it means to be a self, fosters a reaction that marshals the communal self against the alienation and isolation of the individual in a market society. To be sure, the celebration of narrow self-interest is also a reaction against the embedding of the self in community, and its domination by custom, tradition, and social hierarchy. This domination requires that the individual give up (deny or disavow) his or her autonomy, including his or her separateness from the group. Self-development, in which capitalism plays a central role, means that the individual calls into question this claim of the group over his or her identity. The attack on tradition we associate with modernity is about overthrowing the group's claim over the member, which operates through tradition and custom. Thus, modernity opposes tradition, as the particular aspect of the self opposes its universal aspect. The resulting division of the self means that each aspect must appear in a purified, therefore unintegrated, shape appropriate to the absence of its opposing moment: thus, the ongoing conflict between individualist and communitarian notions of justice, one favoring individual right, especially private property, the other favoring group rights.

The self exists in both constructions, in one as the individual, in one as the group. Thus, the communitarian understands the self as the group self. In sharing this self, and making it his or her own, each member becomes not a uniquely particular individual, but a mere instance of the collective identity. While, in the modern context, the group is sometimes democratic, at least in rhetoric, since the communal ideal can be made one of a single, shared, self, it can bring with it a tendency for the community to operate under the domination of a ruler. The shared selfhood of the community becomes the single self of its leader. Because, in the community, there can be only one self, the communal solution often becomes an authoritarian solution, and for reasons bound up with the problem it is meant to solve: the problem of breaking down those self-boundaries perceived to isolate individuals. This is the case outlined earlier, where the universal moment of the self eclipses the particular. The communal solution provides the member with the opportunity to give up the struggle to find and integrate a separate self. This is the opportunity to give the self up to the group (and eventually to the leader). Loss of self into group marks this moment in the process of the development of the self.

Yet, just as loss of self into group can offer an apparent solution to self-alienation, so, especially in the more modern context, can denial of the reality or significance of the community for the individual. This denial is sometimes expressed in the self's aspiration to the pure autonomy of an isolated monad. To protect the self by denying the (significance or integrity) of the other emphasizes the vulnerability of the self to the other, who must be denied, or even destroyed, if the self is to have any hope of surviving. In this case, the particular moment seeks to purge the universal by purging any real dependence on recognition by others, and on connection to a collective self-ideal.

Two solutions, then, mark moments in the history of selfhood: the self in community, where it gives up autonomy and the effort to constitute real self-boundaries as it gives up its self-determination to the whole; and the self in isolation, for whom others do not really exist. Speaking more concretely, we can refer to these as the communal solution and the market solution. There is a sense, of course, in which the two solutions are two sides of the same thing. Each constitutes a singular, unified, selfhood by eliminating all others, one through subordination to the unified self of the community as embodied in its leader, one through the isolation of the individual self separated from a world of selves.

Justice and existing social arrangements

Neither solution advanced above to the dilemma of self-development quite meets the standard of justice because neither solution fully acknowledges the existence of others, and the necessity that we must live with them. The institutions developed around these solutions are not, then, the institutions of justice. However, having said this, it is not clear we have said very much. We can, of course use the concept of justice to rebuke existing social arrangements in the hope that doing so will somehow influence those arrangements in the direction of what is just. But, as I emphasize in Chapter 3, institutions will only be influenced in this way if they are susceptible to the rebuke justice represents for them, which they can only be if they already incorporate the ideal of justice. In other words, the relevance of justice is proportional to the degree in which justice is already established as the animating principle of social life. The more the work of justice in creating its own conditions remains incomplete, the less relevant the ideal of justice will be to altering actually existing arrangements.

One respect in which existing arrangements fall short of justice that I have emphasized has to do with want satisfaction. At various points, I return to the issue of the limitlessness of want and the adequacy of means, that is, the problem of scarcity. This is the historical condition for justice with which political economy has been most closely associated. Our final problem, then, is to link the condition of scarcity to the moments in the development of the self briefly outlined above, thus to link the problem of scarcity to the problem of self-integration. Establishing this connection draws together the main themes that arise in considering justice and the economy. The possibility that we might use the ideal of justice to judge the economy without first adapting that ideal to the condition of scarcity means treating scarcity as a contingent rather than inevitable (especially natural) condition. Linking scarcity to a failure of self-integration would establish the way in which scarcity as an existing condition can be judged by justice rather than limiting what we can hope for in a more just social arrangement.

Scarcity means that want exceeds available means for its satisfaction. We can avoid this condition by assuring that want restricts itself to what is available. This is the message of the classical notion of subsistence, with its emphasis on a moral obligation defined by established ways of life. Scarcity would not be relevant, except by accident, in a world where want was for subsistence. This sort of world erodes with the growth of the market and the multiplication of means. Of course, the multiplication of means must appeal to something within desire for it to dislodge want from its attachment to subsistence. This something is vital since it foreshadows the liberation of want from limits, and thus the development of scarcity. In this development, wealth is both cause and effect, since it corrodes established (finite) ways of life, yet becomes that much more important once those ways of life have begun to break down.

As I suggest in my earlier exploration of subsistence, the limit it represents is the limit of uniformity and fixity of want. Uniformity of want means uniformity of persons, thus a communal rather than an individual reality. The development of individuality as the basis of want means the multiplication of want, the satisfaction of want through exchange, the growth of wealth as the means to want satisfaction, and the loss of want's older limits. But, why does individuation mean that want loses all limit? Why does it not lead to the limitation of want in individual identity? If want were limited by individual identity, so also would the need for wealth be limited. The world organized to satisfy such a want would surely require considerably more wealth than would be otherwise needed (assuming the relevant quantities, which consist of qualitatively different elements, could be compared), but it might still require a finite amount, depending, for example, on the number of persons. This is not, however, the condition that develops when the market and the growth of the individual as source of want undermine the older determination of want in the common subsistence of the group. What additional force has intervened to transform finite want into want without limit, the need for a finite amount of wealth into the pursuit of limitless accumulations, the possibility of satisfaction into a reality of scarcity?

In addition to offering us the means to individuation, and thus to being something finite or particular (which is what we mean by having an identity), wealth seems to offer us freedom from (particular) identity and its limits. It is, after all, the abstractness of wealth that frees us from predetermined ways of life, and allows us to form our own, using our wealth or income in ways peculiar to us. Because we receive our part of the social product first in the form of an abstract claim (money), how that part translates into our way of life is up to us. If we were to receive instead particular goods, for example so much subsistence, then our way of life, so far as that is implicated in what we use and consume, is given to us. Wealth, including its abstract form, then, means freedom from the external determination of identity we associate with subsistence. How does this freedom from the limit defined by the common way of life associated with subsistence lead to freedom from limit itself? The limit in question is the same considered above: the limit of the finite, that is bounded, self.

Self-boundaries establish identity and difference. Self-identity marks limits of what the self is, and therefore what it is not (who we are and who we are not). As I emphasize in Chapter 1, identity also means difference. In a world of different selves, our own self is finite and bounded. These boundaries and limits do not exist for a personhood conceived quantitatively, where each is more or less rather than differently a person, where all are measured on a single scale: wealth. Where personhood is relative and measurable, others represent greater and lesser rather than different selves. Commensurability, by reducing the differences between selves to a matter of amount, establishes a competition over what is, in effect, only one, universal, selfhood. Selfhood is, then, the object of a struggle. Because we cannot all have it in our own way, some will have it and some will not.

For Hegel, this struggle for mastery has its roots in desire (1977, pp. 104-119). Desire is to eliminate the other, or specifically the other's otherness. We cannot tolerate this otherness because it means that we are only one part, something finite and limited, at best one among many and not *the* one. Dominance over the other denies to it the universal status we seek for ourselves alone. Wealth accumulation understood as a path to dominance represents the striving of the particular to be immediately the universal, to blot out all threat that the other's may emerge as the true self, and ours as the diminished and subordinate (dependent) other self. With enough wealth, I can have whatever the other might want or have; and, if only indirectly,

I can be whatever the other is or strives to become.[4] Recall, in this connection, Marx's well-known description of the power of money (1972, pp. 103-5):

> That which is for me through the medium of *money* -- that for which I can pay (i.e. which money can buy) -- that am I, the possessor of money. The extent of the power of money is the extent of my power. Money's properties are my properties and essential powers -- the properties and powers of its possessor. Thus what I *am* and *am capable* of is by no means determined by my individuality. ... That which I am unable to do as a *man*, and which therefore all my individual essential powers are incapable, I am able to do by means of money. ... [M]oney is thus the general overturning of *individualities* ....

Wealth, then, means freedom from self-boundaries as represented in the existence of other selves; or, at least, the pursuit of wealth offers the prospect of such freedom. This prospect is not, however, limited to any one, but available to all. The result is the great struggle to amass wealth in order to become not one among many, but the only one.The struggle to amass wealth without limit expresses the individual's refusal to acknowledge the finiteness of his or her self. Establishing self-limits means recognizing and accepting difference: that the self is not only one but also many.

Advocacy of difference has lately become a major cultural, and, to a lesser degree, political, theme. Just institutions defend difference, and thereby also insist on the limits of the self. Yet, the limits implied in tolerating difference are not always treated as true self-limits, but as limits externally imposed on the self. To this extent, they tend to conflict with the main theme of justice: self-determination.

Limits consistent with justice are limits set by and for the self. With regard to wealth, this means that just institutions do not limit the amount of wealth an individual can want or attain; though they should not exacerbate the individual's impulse to seek security for him or her self in limitless accumulation. In other words, integration means self-interest that already incorporates limits, not one limited from outside. This is the limit implied in being a self among others. Just institutions enable individuals to will their own limits. There can be enough wealth not when wealth is limited externally for the individual, but when that individual loses interest in more wealth than he or she needs to maintain and develop a unique identity.

This solution will, no doubt, seem utopian, not only to those that imagine the desire for wealth to be innate in mankind, but also to those who imagine that desire a mere product of social suggestion. Yet, the utopianism is really on the other side. After all, those who imagine we can limit an aspiration presumed innate by shaping institutions to prevent its expression surely seek a result they themselves deem inconsistent with human nature. And, those who imagine human aspirations can be whatever social institutions shape them to be, in so-doing deny any limits. In this, they are more utopian than any who might argue for the possibility of self-integration as a basis for self-limits.

Dilemmas of justice

The more entrenched the struggle over a unitary selfhood, the more elusive the pursuit of justice. This elusiveness of justice takes the form of dilemmas of justice. By achieving justice along one dimension, we lose it along another. For example, greater adherence to property right assures inequalities that undermine equal opportunity, or equal opportunity demands intrusion on the family that violates its integrity, or steps to enhance the prospects of the least advantaged violate the principle of equal treatment. When we seek to achieve justice within social arrangements not conducive to it, we create dilemmas of this sort.

In light of these dilemmas, it is not surprising to find one student suggesting we give up any unified vision of justice in favor of a 'plurality of principles'. These principles might help define a 'limited liberalism' capable of replacing the vain pursuit of a single ideal of justice free of the dilemmas that, as a practical matter, justice seems unable to avoid (Fishkin 1988, p. 193). The proposal for a limited liberalism, like many suggestions rooted in the debate over distributive justice, insists that we can realize justice in the world more or less as we find it.

For some, justice is an abstract ideal useful as a rebuke to actually existing institutions that are not just. For others, the shape of existing institutions must limit our ideals to assure that we can find those institutions capable of a reasonable degree of justice. Those who use justice to rebuke existing institutions recognize that justice is an ideal, and that we measure what is against our ideals rather than forming ideals according to what exists. Those who argue for a plurality of ideals recognize that only ideals already to a significant degree embedded in the way the world is can have any significance in shaping that world. Neither of the two positions, then, should be ignored. Yet, they clearly conflict, and our problem is to find a way to integrate their (partial) truths.

This problem has an analogue at the level of the individual. To be an individual means to have an identity. Having an identity means having an ideal self (or ego ideal) capable of shaping projects and actions. In this sense, being a person means uniting theory (the ego ideal) and practice (realizing that ideal in an actual way of life). To unify theory and practice in this way, two conditions must be met. First, the ideal must be appropriate to a self, that is, it must incorporate the general ideal of selfhood in a concrete, particular form and setting. Second, the ideal must be capable of being made real; it must be realistic. For example, if to realize my ideal I must dominate others, and in that sense make myself the only self, I will encounter severe obstacles in my effort to make it real. Or, if my ideal falls short of the ideal of being a self, because it incorporates too great a measure of subordination to others and thus loss of self, I might succeed in making it real, but in so-doing I will fail to be a self, since what I will be does not realize the ideal of selfhood.

The ideal of justice encounters this same problem. It must be a true ideal of justice, and it must be an ideal we can make real in the world. The problem becomes a dilemma when its two parts separate so that being a true ideal of justice means being an ideal we cannot make real. One response is to change our ideal to what can be real; the other insists that an ideal far removed from reality can nonetheless remake the world.

For the individual, the problem can only be solved in a world conducive to being a self. If the world is not of this kind, if for example it merges all into the group or makes some the subjects of others, then the problem of being a self cannot be solved. No amount of compromising the ideal of selfhood changes this, nor can the true ideal of selfhood overthrow the reality antithetical to it. If, however, the world is conducive to being a self, or at least reasonably so, then the individual's problem can be solved by altering his or her self-ideal into one capable of being made real.

An unjust order will not be made just by being placed in the bright light of justice's ideal. But, having an ideal of justice that can become real is a precondition for realizing justice where its conditions are already well enough established. The problem is the role justice plays, and the means it employs, in setting its own foundation by fostering the development of those conditions it requires if it is to be real. This is the problem of the presence and absence of justice we refer to as its development.

Implementing justice

Implementing justice is nothing like curing cancer. The successful cancer researcher might expect his or her research to be used to alleviate suffering, to replace less effective methods and those that turn out to do more harm than good. For justice, ineffective and harmful interpretations cannot be so easily displaced, nor can the policies stemming from them. On the contrary, in the realm of justice, the false ideas and harmful policies continue to dominate, and in part because they are false, and do harm.

The two solutions to the problem of failed self-integration discussed above each has an interpretation of justice linked with it. The self in isolation interprets justice as a set of laws preventing any uninvited interaction. The self in community interprets justice as the protection of the communal ideal that subordinates the individual member, sometimes through an attack on difference associated with equality as sameness. As I suggest, neither interpretation successfully integrates the universal and particular aspects of the self; and thus neither enables us to live with others in the strong sense attributed to that idea in this essay. Each interpretation, in its way, does harm to the ideal of justice as living with others; yet, each can call on an army of followers that would overwhelm the more modest claims of justice's ideal to our hopes and expectations.

The problem lies in the split between the two interpretations. Splitting opposes and polarizes what are connected aspects or moments of a single idea, so that thinking takes on an either/or quality: freedom as autonomous willing, or determination of the individual within a larger reality of culture and community given to him. The nature of the split, the involvement of the two moments, the pole that is acknowledged and the pole denied, vary significantly not only with level of development, but also with culture and history. Thus, in some contexts, the moment of will dominates, and seeks to deny the limits set by the existence of others, including the group. In other contexts, the moment of group identity dominates, and seeks to root out the separation of persons into unique units.

In the United States, as is often observed, the moment of the will in isolation tends to dominate. Thus, following the Puritans, social policy in America institutes the idea summarized by the dictum that, to paraphrase R.H. Tawney, will is all, circumstance nothing (Tawney 1962, p. 230). Here, the poor are poor because they are unwilling to be anything else. If this is the case, then the worst thing we can do for them is to provide assistance that might undermine their will. Instead, social policy is designed to force the poor to will their own escape from poverty, or act as if they could do so, or suffer the consequences if they fail. Critics of the prevailing attitude counter with the idea that will is nothing, circumstance all; the poor are poor because they are deprived by others of the opportunity to be anything else. For the critic, will is an illusion; what the individual does or does not accomplish is not a matter of inner resources and capacities, but of opportunity afforded by the group. We can only imagine, then, either self-determination as isolated willing, or social determination as external imposition.

The justice of the isolated will offers the prospect that nothing can impede the individual in the pursuit of his or her ends other than a failure of will ('Just say no to drugs'). The American experience organizes itself around the idea that there are no limits to individual attainment other than those within the individual him or her self. The limits of circumstance and the world as it can be operate weakly if at all on the hopes we might entertain in this world, where, for example, there is no limit to the wealth we can accumulate if we have the talent, ambition, and luck.

The justice of the self in community, by contrast, seems to offer little, and to accept that living with others sharply restricts what we can have for ourselves. Yet, in its way, it offers an even greater bounty: merger into the group, and the integration of self offered by taking on a group identity. The limitless aspiration of those who believe in the power of individual will is shifted from the individual to the group. However limited the individual in what he or she can have as his or her own, no such limit restricts the group, which, as Freud remarks, is a place where 'the notion of impossibility disappears' (Freud 1959, p. 9).

It might be said, then, that our two solutions to the problem of self-integration share an important quality: they each, if in different ways, deny limits. This denial of limits is clearly expressed in the demand for justice, which in its usual meaning, insists that a loss be put right, and which, therefore, assumes that loss can be put right. This idea that loss can be put right is the great myth of justice, and the source of the power it has over us. To implement justice, however, we must give to justice a more modest purpose, one that, unlike righting wrong, can be realized in the world. Yet, to give justice this more modest goal, we must first give up the interpretations of justice that arise out of the splitting apart of the moments of the self, each of which insists that a power can be called upon capable of setting right what has gone wrong: the failed integration of the self into a unit. Whether this is the power of the individual will or of the group, insisting that we call upon it to realize justice makes that task one we can never accomplish. We can only implement a justice that seeks not to right a past wrong, or replace what we have lost, but to prevent the further imposition of loss, and secure the possibility that we might be ourselves in the world.

Notes

1 An understanding perhaps derived from Hegel's *Philosophy of History* (1956).

2 For a discussion of this emphasis in the idea of progress, see Habermas (1984, part II).

3 The classic reference is Hegel (1977).

4 These considerations may shed some light on John Rawls's elliptical justification for the scarcity assumption (1971, p. 119): 'Now obviously no one can obtain everything he wants; the mere existence of other persons prevents this.'

Bibliography

Adamson, Walter (1990), 'Economic Democracy and the Expediency of Worker Participation', *Political Studies*, Vol. 38, No. 1, March.

Anderson, Elizabeth (1990), 'The Ethical Limitations of the Market', *Economics and Philosophy*, Vol. 6, No. 2.

Apprey, Maurice and Howard Stein (1993), *Intersubjectivity, Projective Identification, and Otherness*, Duquesne University Press: Pittsburgh.

Arendt, Hanna (1958), *The Human Condition*, University of Chicago Press: Chicago.

Arrow, Kenneth (1951), *Social Choice and Individual Values*, Yale University Press: New Haven.

Avineri, Shlomo (1969), *The Social and Political Thought of Karl Marx*, Cambridge University Press: Cambridge.

Baker, Dean (1992), 'The Right to Income', *Journal of Income Distribution*, Vol. 2, No.1, Summer.

Baran, Paul (1957), *The Political Economy of Growth*, Monthly Review Press: New York.

___ and Paul Sweezy (1966), *Monopoly Capital*, Monthly Review Press: New York.

Barry, Brian (1989), *Theory of Justice*, University of California Press: Berkeley.

Beitz, Charles (1985), 'Justice and International Relations', in Beitz, Charles (ed.), *International Ethics*, Princeton University Press: Princeton.

Benhabib, Seyla (1992), *Situating the Self: Gender, Community, and Postmodernism in Contemporary Ethics*, Routledge: London.

Benjamin, Jessica (1992), 'Recognition and Destruction: An Outline of Intersubjectivity', in Skolnick, Neil and Susan Warshaw (eds.), *Relational Perspectives in Psychoanalysis*, The Analytic Press: Hillsdale N.J.

Blaney, David (1994), 'Cultural Neutrality and the Emergence of

International Governance', paper presented to the Meetings of the American Political Science Association, New York.
Blaney, David and Naeem Inayatullah (forthcoming), 'IPE as a Culture of Competition', in Jacquin, D., A. Oros, and M. Verweij (eds.), *Culture in World Politics*, MacMillan: London.
Bollas, Christopher (1989), *Forces of Destiny*, Free Association Press: London.
Brenkert, George (1992), 'Freedom, Participation and Corporations: The Issue of Corporate (Economic) Democracy', *Business Ethics Quarterly*, Vol. 2, No. 3.
Brittan, Samuel 1989, ' "The Economic Contradictions of Democracy" Revisited', *The Political Quarterly*, Vol. 60, No. 2, April.
Buchanan, James and Gordon Tulloch (1962), *The Calculus of Consent*, University of Michigan Press: Ann Arbor.
Bull, Hedley, (1977), *Anarchical Society*, Columbia University Press: New York.
Caporaso, James and David Levine (1992), *Theories of Political Economy*, Cambridge University Press: New York.
Chasseguet-Smirgel, Janine (1985), *The Ego Ideal*, Norton: New York.
Cohen, G.A. (1979), 'The Labor Theory of Value and the Concept of Exploitation', *Philosophy and Public Affairs*, Vol. 8, No. 4, Summer.
Dahl, Robert (1956), *A Preface to Democratic Theory*, University of Chicago Press: Chicago.
___ (1985), *A Preface to Economic Democracy*, University of California Press: Berkeley.
Desmond, William (1987), *Desire, Dialectic, and Otherness*, Yale University Press: New Haven.
Dewey, John (1939), *Freedom and Culture*, G.P. Putnam's Sons: New York.
Diamond, Larry (1992), 'Economic Development and Democracy Reconsidered', *American Behavioral Scientist*, Vol. 35, No. 4/5, March/June.
Durkheim, Emile (1958), *Professional Ethics and Civic Morals*, Brookfield, Cornelia (tr.), The Free Press: Glencoe, Il.
___ (1984), *The Division of Labor in Society*, The Free Press: New York.
Dworkin, Ronald (1977), *Taking Rights Seriously*, Harvard University Press: Cambridge, Ma.
Erikson, Erik (1956), 'The Problem of Ego Identity', *Journal of the American Psychoanalytic Association*, Vol. 4, No. 1, January.
Fairbairn, W. Ronald (1952), *Psychoanalytic Studies of the Personality*, Routledge & Kegan Paul: London.
Fishkin, James (1988), *Justice, Equal Opportunity, and the Family*, Yale University Press: New Haven.
Fitzgerald, Francis (1986), *Cities on a Hill: A Journey Through Contemporary American Cultures*, Simon and Schuster Inc: New York.

Freud, Sigmund (1959), *Group Psychology and the Analysis of the Ego*, W.W. Norton: New York.
Furman, Erna (1980), 'Early Latency–Normal and Pathological Aspects', in Greenspan, S.J. and G.H. Pollock, (eds), *The Course of Life: Psychoanalytic Contributions toward Understanding Personality Development*, Vol. II. NIMH.
Geertz, Clifford (1963), 'The Integrative Revolution', Geertz, C. (ed), *Old Societies and New States*, The Free Press: New York.
Ginsberg, Morris (1965), *On Justice in Society* Cornell University Press: Ithaca.
Greenberg, Jay and Stephen Mitchell (1983), *Object Relations in Psychoanalytic Theory*, Harvard University Press: Cambridge, Ma.
Habermas, Jurgen (1984), *The Theory of Communicative Action*, Volume I, McCarthy, T. (ed.), Beacon Press: Boston.
Hegel, G.W.F. (1951), *Hegel's Philosophy of Right*, Knox, T.M. (tr.), Oxford University Press: Oxford.
___ (1956), *The Philosophy of History*, Sibree, J. (tr.), Dover Publications: New York.
___ (1977), *Hegel's Phenomenology of Spirit*, Miller, A.V. (tr.), Oxford University Press: Oxford.
Heilbroner, Robert (1985), *The Nature and Logic of Capitalism*, W.W. Norton: New York.
Hirst, Paul (1991) 'The State, Civil Society and the Collapse of Soviet Communism', *Economy and Society*, Vol. 20, No. 2, May.
Jevons, William S. (1988), *The Theory of Political Economy*. MacMillan: London.
Keohane, Robert (1984), *Beyond Hegemony: Co-operation and Discord in the World Political Economy*, Princeton University Press: Princeton.
Khan, M. Masud R. (1974), *The Privacy of the Self*, International Universities Press: New York.
Kindleberger, Charles (1973), *The World in Depression, 1929-1939*. Allen Lane: London.
Kohut, Heinz (1977), *The Restoration of the Self*, International Universities Press: New York.
Krasner, Stephen (1978), *Defending the National Interest*, Princeton University Press: Princeton.
Lafontaine, J.S. (1985), 'Person and Individual: Some Anthropological Reflections', in Carrithers, M. (ed), *The Category of the Person*, Cambridge University Press: Cambridge.
Laing, R.D. (1965), *The Divided Self*, Penguin Books: London.
Levine, David P. (1977), *Economic Studies*. Routledge & Kegan Paul: London.
___ (1978), *Economic Theory*, Vol. I., Routledge and Kegan Paul: London.
___ (1982), 'The Determinants of Capitalist Expansion', *Economic*

Development and Cultural Change, Vol. 31, No. 2, January.
Levine, David P. (1988), *Needs, Rights, and the Market*, Lynne Rienner Publishers: Boulder.
___ (1989), 'The Sense of Theory in Political Economy', *Rethinking Marxism*, Vol. 2, No. 1, Spring.
___ (1992), 'The Concept of Subsistence in Classical Economics', *Journal of Income Distribution*, Vol. 2, No. 1, Summer.
___ (1995), *Wealth and Freedom*, Cambridge University Press: New York.
___ (1996), 'Diversity, Autonomy, and Citizenship', *The Good Society* Vol. 6, No. 2, Spring.
___ (1998), *Subjectivity in Political Economy*, London: Routledge.
Lewis, W. Arthur (1978), *The Evolution of International Economic Order*, Princeton University Press: Princeton.
Lienhardt, Godfrey (1985), 'Self: Public, Private. Some African Representations', in Carrithers, M. (ed), *The Category of the Person*, Cambridge University Press: Cambridge.
Lindblom, C.E. (1977), *Politics and Markets*, Basic Books: New York.
Maker, William (1994), *Philosophy without Foundations*, SUNY Press: Albany.
Manzas, Jeff (1992), 'Postindustrial Capitalism, the State, and the Prospects for Economic Democracy', *Journal of Political and Military Sociology*, Vol. 20 No. 2.
Marx, Karl (1967), *Capital*, Vol 1, International Publishers: New York.
___ (1972), *The Marx-Engels Reader*, Tucker, R. (ed), W.W. Norton: New York.
Mauss, Marcel (1985), 'A Category of the Human Mind: the Notion of Person; the Notion of Self', Halls, W.D. (tr.), in Carrithers, M. (ed.), *The Category of the Person*, Cambridge University Press: Cambridge.
Miller, David (1976), *Social Justice*, Oxford University Press, Oxford.
Mitchell, Stephen (1993), *Hope and Dread in Psychoanalysis*, Basic Books: New York.
Murphy, Raymond (1988), *Social Closure: The Theory of Monopolies and Exclusion*, Clarendon Press: Oxford.
Nardin, Terry (1983), *Law, Morality, and the Relations of States*, Princeton University Press: Princeton.
Nozick, Robert (1974), *Anarchy, State, and Utopia*, Harvard University Press: Cambridge, Ma.
Offe, Claus (1987) 'Challenging the Boundaries of Institutional Politics: Social Movements since the 1960s', in Maier, Charles (ed.), *Changing Boundaries of the Political*, Cambridge University Press: Cambridge.
Ogden, Thomas (1986), *The Matrix of the Mind*, Jason Aronson Inc: Northvale, N.J.

Okun, Arthur (1975), *Equality and Efficiency*, Brookings: Washington, D.C.
Pateman, Carole (1970), *Participation and Democratic Theory*, Cambridge University Press: Cambridge.
Perez-Diaz, Victor (1993), 'Civil Society and the State: Rise and Fall of the State as Bearer of a Moral Project', *The Tocqueville Review*, Vol. 14, No. 1.
Pleydell, Alan (1982), 'Language, Culture and the Concept of International Political Community', in Mayall, J. (ed.) *The Community of States*, George Allen & Unwin: London.
Rawls, John (1971), *A Theory of Justice*, Harvard University Press: Cambridge, Ma.
Ricardo, David (1951), *Works and Correspondence of David Ricardo*, Vol. 1, Sraffa, P. (ed.), Cambridge University Press: Cambridge.
Sahlins, Marshall (1972), *Stoneage Economics*, Aldine: Chicago.
Sandel, Michael (1982), *Liberalism and the Limits of Justice*, Cambridge University Press: Cambridge.
Sandler, Joseph (1987), *From Safety to Superego*, Guilford: New York.
Sassower, Raphael (1993), *Knowledge without Expertise*, SUNY Press: Albany.
Schafer, Roy (1981), *A New Language for Psychoanalysis*, Yale University Press: New Haven.
___ (1983), *The Analytic Attitude*, Basic Books: New York.
Schecter, Roberta (1992), 'Voice of a Hidden Minority: Identification and Countertransference in the Cross-Cultural Working Alliance', *American Journal of Psychoanalysis*, Vol. 52, No. 4.
Schelling, Thomas (1984), 'Economic Reasoning and the Ethics of Policy', in *Choice and Consequence*, Harvard University Press: Cambridge, Ma.
Schumpeter, Joseph A. (1950), *Capitalism, Socialism, and Democracy*, Harper and Row: New York.
Sen, A K (1977), 'Rational Fools: A Critique of the Behavioral Assumptions of Economic Theory', *Philosophy and Public Affairs*, Vol. 6.
Shapiro, David (1981), *Autonomy and Rigid Character*, Basic Books: New York.
Shapiro, Nina (1994), 'Ownership and Management,' in Davidson, P. and J. Kregel (eds.), *Employment, Growth, and Finance*, Edward Elgar: Aldershot, Hants.
Smith, Adam (1969), *The Theory of Moral Sentiments*, Liberty Classics: Indianapolis.
___ (1937), *The Wealth of Nations*, Modern Library: New York.
Sraffa, Piero (1960), *Production of Commodities by Means of Commodities*, Cambridge University Press: Cambridge.
Stern, Daniel (1985), *The Interpersonal World of the Infant*, Basic Books: New

York.

Stirati, Antonella (1994), *The Theory of Wages in Classical Economics*, Edward Elgar: Aldershot, Hants.

Strange, Susan (1987), 'The Persistent Myth of Lost Hegemony', *International Organization*, Vol. 41 No. 4, Autumn.

Tawney, R.H. (1962), *Religion and the Rise of Capitalism*, Peter Smith: Gloucester.

Taylor, Charles (1982), 'The Diversity of Goods', in Sen, A. and B. Williams, (eds), *Utilitarianism and Beyond*, Cambridge University Press: Cambridge.

___ (1985), 'The Person', in Carrithers, M. (ed), *The Category of the Person*, Cambridge University Press: Cambridge.

Todorov, Tsvetan (1993), *On Human Diversity*, Harvard University Press: Cambridge, Ma.

Umari, Nawfal (1992), 'Subsistence and Development', *The Journal of Income Distribution*, Vol. 2, No. 1, Summer.

Volkan, Vamik (1988), *The Need to Have Enemies and Allies*, Jason Aronson, Inc.: Northvale, N.J.

von Broembsen, F. (1989), 'Transformations of Identity: Referent Location, Agency, and Levels of Integration in the Progress from Potential Self to Existential Identity', *American Journal of Psychoanalysis*, Vol. 49, No. 4., December.

Walker, R.B.J. (1993), *Inside/Outside: International Relations as Political Theory*, Cambridge University Press: Cambridge.

Walzer, Michael (1983), *Spheres of Justice*, Basic Books: New York.

___ (1986), 'Toward a Theory of Social Assignments', in Knowlton, W. and R. Zeckhauser (eds.), *American Society: Public and Private Responsibilities*, Ballinger: Cambridge, Ma.

Williams, Bernard (1962), 'The Idea of Equality', in P. Laslett and W.G. Runciman (eds), *Philosophy, Politics, and Society*, Second Series, Oxford University Press: Oxford.

Winfield, Richard D. (1988a), *The Just Economy*, Routledge: London.

___ (1988b), *Reason and Justice*, SUNY Press: Albany.

___ (1988c), 'Hegel Versus the New Orthodoxy', in Desmond, W. (ed), *Hegel and His Critics*, SUNY Press: Albany.

___ (1991), *Freedom and Modernity*, SUNY Press: Albany.

Winnicott, D.W. (1965), 'Ego Distortion in terms of True and False Self', reprinted in *The Maturational Process and the Facilitating Environment*, International Universities Press: New York.

___ (1974), *Playing and Reality*, Penguin: Middlesex, England.

___ (1988), *Human Nature*, Schocken: New York.

Wood, Allen (1972), 'The Marxian Critique of Justice', *Philosophy and Public Affairs*, Vol. 1, No. 3, Spring.

Yeatman, Anna (1994), *Postmodern Revisionings of the Political*, Routledge:

London.

Young, Iris (1990), *Justice and the Politics of Difference*, Princeton University Press: Princeton.

Zucker, Ross (1995), 'Whose Property is it Anyway? The Social Nature of Economic Actors and Egalitarian Remuneration', *Review of Political Economy*, Vol. 7, No. 4, October.

Index

For Product Safety Concerns and Information please contact our EU representative GPSR@taylorandfrancis.com Taylor & Francis Verlag GmbH, Kaufingerstraße 24, 80331 München, Germany

Batch number: 10725909

Printed by Printforce, the Netherlands